Y0-BGA-321

FT LEAVENWORTH, KS   66027

Just War and Vatican Council II: A Critique

by Robert W. Tucker

WITH COMMENTARY BY

George G. Higgins
Ralph Potter
Richard H. Cox
Paul Ramsey

Published by

The Council on Religion and International Affairs

WITHDRAWN

HIEBERT LIBRARY
FRESNO PACIFIC UNIV.-M. B. SEMINARY
FRESNO CA 93702

Ethics and Foreign Policy Series (50¢ each)

ETHICS AND NATIONAL PURPOSE
Kenneth W. Thompson

MORALITY AND MODERN WAR
John Courtney Murray, S.J.

RELIGION AND INTERNATIONAL RESPONSIBILITY
Robert Gordis

THE RECOVERY OF ETHICS
Paul H. Nitze

THE MORALITY AND POLITICS OF INTERVENTION
Manfred Halpern

THE LIMITS OF NUCLEAR WAR:
THINKING ABOUT THE DO-ABLE AND THE UN-DO-ABLE
Paul Ramsey

AN ALTERNATIVE TO WAR
Gordon Zahn

MORAL TENSIONS IN INTERNATIONAL AFFAIRS
John C. Bennett

SOUTH AFRICA: PROBLEMS AND PROSPECTS
Philip W. Quigg
with commentary by J. S. F. Botha, Kenneth Carstens, Vernon McKay

FOREIGN AID: MORAL AND POLITICAL ASPECTS
Victor C. Ferkiss

JUST WAR AND VATICAN COUNCIL II: A CRITIQUE
Robert W. Tucker
with commentary by George G. Higgins, Ralph Potter, Richard Cox,
Paul Ramsey

COUNTERINSURGENCY: SOME PROBLEMS AND IMPLICATIONS
Edgar S. Furniss, Jr.
with commentary by Charles Burton Marshall, William V. O'Brien

THE U.S. IN ASIA: EVOLUTION AND CONTAINMENT
David P. Mozingo

MODERN WAR AND THE PURSUIT OF PEACE
Theodore R. Weber

Special Studies

THE MORAL DILEMMA OF NUCLEAR WEAPONS: ESSAYS FROM *worldview*
William Clancy, ed. $1.50

PEACE, THE CHURCHES AND THE BOMB
James Finn, ed. $2.00

NUCLEAR WEAPONS: CAN THEIR SPREAD BE HALTED?
Betty Goetz Lall 50¢

THE U. S. AND WARS OF NATIONAL LIBERATION: REPORT ON A SEMINAR
Quentin L. Quade 50¢

U.S. POLICY IN THE FAR EAST: IDEOLOGY, RELIGION AND SUPERSTITION
Kenneth W. Thompson, Hans J. Morgenthau, Jerald C. Brauer $1.75

AMERICAN FOREIGN POLICY AND MORAL RHETORIC
David Little $1.75

THE RIGHT TO KNOW, TO WITHHOLD AND TO LIE
William J. Barnds
with commentary by Wilson Carey McWilliams, Daniel C. Maguire,
Paul W. Blackstock $1.75

ETHICS, VIOLENCE AND REVOLUTION
Charles C. West
with commentary by Ernest W. Lefever, Monika Hellwig $1.75

Copyright 1966 by
THE COUNCIL ON RELIGION AND INTERNATIONAL AFFAIRS
170 East 64th Street, New York, N. Y. 10021
Third Printing 1970

All rights reserved
Printed in the United States of America
Library of Congress No. 66-28407

FOREWORD

This booklet appears as one in a series devoted to "Ethics and Foreign Policy." This series argues for no single point of view; it is in fact expressly designed to draw upon the various great traditions, moral and political, which are our common heritage and from which we derive frequently diverse conclusions. The essays are united, however, in their essential concern, for each attempts to relate religious and moral insight to contemporary events so that the possibilities of an ordered justice may be more nearly perceived.

The conditions of modern warfare have impelled many people to a reconsideration of traditional theories of *bellum justum*, the just war. Some have found concepts of the just war to have contemporary relevance; others have questioned whether they are currently applicable to the full range of modern weapons systems.

Since the statements on war which were made by the Second Vatican Council derived from a tradition in which just-war concepts are pervasive, it seemed useful to subject these statements to a critique in the light of *bellum justum* as it is variously understood. The resulting discussion, it was judged, should clarify the differences and advance the state of the question. This, in fact, is exactly what took place at one of CRIA's regularly scheduled consultations at which Robert W. Tucker presented the paper which initiated the discussion.

Robert W. Tucker is a member of the Committee on International Studies, the Johns Hopkins University, and a member of the Washington Center of Foreign Policy Research. Much of the material in this essay appears in a book published by the Johns Hopkins Press, *Force, Order and Justice*, of which Mr. Tucker and Robert E. Osgood are co-authors.

The Rt. Rev. Msgr. George G. Higgins is director of the Social Action Department of the United States Catholic Conference. He was a frequent member of the press panel in Rome that gave expert opinion on the activities of Vatican Council II while it was in session.

3

Ralph Potter is professor of social ethics, Harvard Divinity School.

Richard H. Cox is a member of the Department of Political Science, State University of New York, Buffalo, New York.

Paul Ramsey is Harrington Spear Paine Professor of Christian Ethics at Princeton University. Among his many publications are *War and the Christian Conscience,* and *The Just War: Force and Political Responsibility.*

JAMES FINN
Director of Publications

Council on Religion and
International Affairs

CONTENTS

Foreword   3

Just War and Vatican Council II:
A Critique   7
by Robert W. Tucker

     Modern Versions of the Just War   7

     The Means of War; Do Limits Exist?   19

     The Just War and the Vatican Council   39

The Pastoral *Constitution*   51
by George G. Higgins

Just War and Reasons of State   53
by Ralph Potter

Which Version of Just War?   62
by Richard H. Cox

Tucker's Bellum contra Bellum Justum   67
by Paul Ramsey

BELLUM JUSTUM AND THE SECOND VATICAN COUNCIL: A CRITIQUE

by Robert W. Tucker

Our task in this paper is to examine the position on war and deterrence taken by the Second Vatican Council and to do so against the background of a general inquiry into efforts to adapt the doctrine of *bellum justum* to the nuclear age.

The significance of *bellum justum* is that in the history of Western thought it has formed the principal alternative to the ancient plea of necessity or reason of state. If the latter emanates from the state itself, the former has a source that is independent of and presumably superior to the state and its necessities. If the argument of necessity places no inherent restraints on the measures that may be taken to secure the state's independence and continuity, the doctrine of *bellum justum* insists that there are such inherent restraints—inherent not in the sense that they may not in fact be exceeded but in the sense that there can be no justification for ever exceeding them. Nevertheless, the observance of these restraints, whatever the circumstances, is not equated with the renunciation of statecraft. Now as in the past, the doctrine of *bellum justum* does not attempt to deal with the critical issue of means simply by abandoning statecraft. In most of its contemporary versions, as in its traditional versions, it seeks instead to square the circle by acknowledging that the state has its necessities and at the same time by insisting that the measures by which these necessities may be preserved must remain limited.

Modern Versions of the Just War

In considering contemporary versions of *bellum justum* it must be immediately observed that with respect to the justification for resorting to force there is little to distinguish these versions from contemporary developments elsewhere, notably developments in international law. Both in contemporary international law as well as in the prevailing twentieth century reconstruction of *bellum justum* war is no longer a means generally permitted to states for the redress of rights that have been violated. Still less is war considered a legitimate means for changing the *status quo*. To the extent that armed force remains a means permitted to states, it does so only to protect the state's self—its territorial integrity and political independence—against unjust attack.[1]

This restriction of the right of recourse to war in modern versions of *bellum justum* has been represented as a far-reaching change from the classic doctrine, though as we shall presently see the precise significance of the change is dependent upon the meaning and scope accorded to legitimate self-defense. In the classic doctrine the just war was a war of execution, an act of vindicative justice, taken to punish an offending state for a wrong done and unamended. But the rights in defense of which, or for the vindication of which, the traditional doctrine permitted states to resort to war, when alternative means of self-redress proved unavailing and unsatisfactory, were not restricted to the right of self-defense. Indeed, the "blameless self-defense" of the classic doctrine represented only one cause justifying the resort to war, and a cause the justice of which appeared so self-evident to the expositors of the doctrine as to scarcely warrant discussion. The primary concern was rather with the problem of "aggressive" or offensive war (i.e., aggressive or offensive in the sense of the initiation of force). The broad response of the classic doctrine to this problem was simply that aggressive war was justified when undertaken by constituted authority, with right intention and as a last resort, to restore the order of justice violated by the offending state.

If it is nevertheless said that the classic doctrine of *bellum justum* was, in principle, defensive, it was so in the sense that war was to be undertaken in defense of justice. It clearly was not defensive in any other sense; at least, it was not necessarily defensive. Not only was aggressive war permitted to redress an injury, to enforce one's rights, it was also permitted to forestall injurious action. The *bellum justum* could thus comprise a preventive war. Yet the "order of justice" in the defense of which aggressive or offensive war could be taken was

---

[1] The above statements no more than summarize the contemporary *jus ad bellum*. Some of the complexities and persisting ambiguities that attend this development are discussed in succeeding pages. Here it is sufficient simply to note that the formulation given in the text appears to represent the present consensus of Catholic and Protestant thought. The right of self-defense against unjust attack is complemented by the right of collective defense, i.e., the right of third parties to come to the defense of the party acting in legitimate self-defense.

never apparent. The rights in defense of which, or for the vindication of which, states might resort to war remained obscure, even among the expositors of the doctrine. Comprising both legal and natural rights, the just war in the classic doctrine was a war waged to enforce both positive and natural law. But there was no more assurance in an earlier era than today that law and justice would always coincide, despite the contrary assumptions of the classic doctrine.[2] When they did not, states might choose between the two. If the identification of positive right and its violation has always proven difficult, the identification of natural right in terms of the conflicting claims and aspirations of states has proven far more difficult. Given the circumstances in which they were applied, these features of the classic doctrine could scarcely constitute a serious restraint on state action. The criticism that has always been made with such telling effect against the argument of necessity may be made with equal effect against these features of the classic doctrine of *bellum justum*. As a justification of war the latter clearly must invite as much abuse at the hands of governments—and, it is only fair to add, not only at the hands of governments—as does the former. In this respect, at least, the contrast often drawn between *bellum justum* and reason of state seems unpersuasive; the one appears no less, or no more, subject to abuse than does the other.[3]

------

[2] The classic doctrine assumed not only the harmony of law and justice but the coincidence of peace and justice. In this view, peace is an ordered concord based upon justice. That a choice might have to be made between law and justice, on the one hand, or between peace and justice, on the other hand, was excluded by the classic doctrine. This equation of peace, order and justice continues to characterize contemporary versions of *bellum justum*, although it can scarcely be said to carry the same conviction today.

[3] It is significant that in a vast literature devoted to the problem of war in Christian thought, and particularly to the doctrine of *bellum justum,* there has been so little inquiry into the relation of doctrine to practice. It is only in recent years, and for recent wars, that such inquiry has been increasingly undertaken. For the most part, however, the literature of pure exegesis on *bellum justum* is as abundant as the literature on the practical uses to which the doctrine has been put in statecraft is scarce. That the doctrine has been abused on numerous occasions over the centuries, that it has been invoked time and again to justify policies of aggrandizement, is scarcely open to dispute. It may of course be argued that these abuses are without relevance to the intrinsic merits of the doctrine. But if this argument is employed in the case of *bellum justum* it must also be applied in the case of reason of state. To confront the theory of the one with the practice of the other clearly will not do. We can only assume that the historical fate of *bellum justum* forms as much a commentary on the doctrine as the historical fate of reason of state forms a commentary on the argument of necessity.

There is no need to labor the considerations that have prompted the change in the twentieth century reconstruction of *bellum justum*. In the main, the restriction of the just war to the war of self-defense rests on the presumption that war can no longer serve as an apt and proportionate means for resolving international conflicts. That presumption, in turn, presumably reflects our contemporary experience with war. There are dissenters from this reconstruction of the classic doctrine.[4] Their objections to restricting the just war to a war of self-defense are not unlike the objections raised by a number of jurists to restricting the legal war to a war of self-defense. In the absence of a society possessed of effective collective procedures for protecting the rights of its members as well as for changing conditions that have become oppressive and inequitable, it is argued that the attempt to deny states this ultimate means of self-redress—save as a measure of self-defense against attack—is bound to fail. Nor is it clear, in the view of some, that the attempt to proscribe "aggressive" war ought even to succeed, and this despite the destructiveness of war in this century, so long as those conditions persist that have always marked international society.[5] Whatever the merits of this view, and it is not to be lightly dismissed, the dominant position today is that armed force is forbidden except as a measure of legitimate self-defense.[6]

---

[4] Thus Paul Ramsey writes: "No sweeping proscription of 'aggressive' war can hope to stand, based as it is on the assumption that history can be frozen where we are, i.e., always in a relatively unjust *pax-ordo* or on the entirely erroneous assumption that any existing international organization is capable of introducing *fundamental* change into this order but in an entirely orderly fashion and by mutual consent. And in any case, aggression has to be defined so as to include within its meaning, not only the first resort to arms, but also any basic challenge to the security of a rival nation, to its *pax-ordo-justitia* and the laws of its peace, against which the only effective defense may be, and is known to be, a resort to armed force." *War and the Christian Conscience* (1961), pp. 89–90.

[5] The most persuasive presentation of the above view is the work of Julius Stone, *Aggression and World Order* (1958).

[6] These summary remarks on a critically important—if ultimately insoluble —controversy warrant some further discussion. Quite apart from the central question of the scope and meaning to be given "legitimate self-defense," this proscription of "aggressive" wars in the twentieth century reconstruction of *bellum justum* must encounter two difficulties. On the one hand, it can not be understood to imply that defensive wars are necessarily just wars. Clearly, the principle of proportionality applies to wars of "legitimate self-defense" as well, whatever the scope and meaning to be given the latter. Even a defensive war may not be an "apt and proportionate means"; even a defensive war, then, may be an unjust war if the good secured by such a war is outweighed by the evil attendant upon—or expected to attend—the conduct of war. This is precisely the

10

Does this change with respect to the justification for resorting to war permit a more persuasive contrast to be drawn today between *bellum justum* and reason of state than could be drawn in an earlier era? Does the twentieth century reconstruction of *bellum justum* thereby limit the "necessities" of the state in a way that the classic doctrine did not? The answer to these questions evidently depends largely upon the manner in which current versions of *bellum justum* circumscribe this one remaining cause justifying war. In fact, however, current versions of *bellum justum* do not appear to have a great

---

issue raised by the prospect of thermonuclear war; even if defensive in character, a thermonuclear war may nevertheless be an unjust war. On the other hand, if a defensive war may nevertheless be an unjust war, it does not necessarily follow from the principle of proportionality that under present conditions an "aggressive" war must be an unjust war. The presumption is not self-evident that war—any and all war—can no longer serve as an apt and proportionate means for resolving international conflicts. (Nor, for that matter, is it self-evident that war —any and all war—can no longer be waged with "right intent" and the proper means.) To say this is not at all to dismiss our experience with war in this century; it is simply to say that despite this experience, and despite the possible consequences of thermonuclear war, there may still be wars and wars. Our experience is neither so unambiguous nor our future so certain as to warrant making what is in effect an irrebuttable presumption. In his celebrated encyclical *Pacem in Terris*, John XXIII spoke of the "cruel destruction and the immense suffering" which the use of modern arms would bring to humanity and for this reason declared that "it is irrational to believe that war is still an apt means of vindicating violated rights." In taking this position John XXIII followed his predecessor, Pius XII, who also condemned the theory that war could serve today as an apt and proportionate means of state policy. Yet it is clearly quite possible to imagine that war might still serve in certain circumstances as an apt and proportionate means to repair injustice, although technically such a war would be an "aggressive" war. Moreover, as noted above, if the "aggressive" resort to armed force is always to be condemned on the basis of its disproportionality, the justice of defensive wars must also be seriously questioned. It is another matter to argue that while there may still be just "aggressive" wars, to proscribe any and all aggressive wars is nevertheless desirable given the conditions that have always attended the use of force in international society. On this view, whatever may be the merits of a particular case, the sum of our experience indicates that given these conditions force is more likely to promote injustice than justice, and that this expectation is very considerably strengthened by the novel conditions presently attending the use of force. The parallel argument in law must be that to permit states the right to use force as a measure of self-help to redress violations—or, rather, alleged violations—of their rights is more likely to promote disorder than order. It must be admitted, however, that this particular argument—whether undertaken on the moral or legal level—is inconclusive, even under present conditions. It depends, among other things, upon an interpretation of the history of state relations, past and present, that leaves ample room for uncertainty and disagreement.

11

deal to say about the meaning and scope of this one remaining justification for war. What they do have to say does not differ substantially
from the more extended and detailed juristic analyses of the right of
self-defense. In consequence, the same difficulties and ambiguities
marking the concept of self-defense in contemporary international law
also mark the concept of self-defense in most current versions of
bellum justum. In the latter no less than in the former uncertainty and
controversy persist over the vital issues of the rights on behalf of
which, and the acts in response to which, forcible measures of self-
defense may be undertaken.

The principal reasons for this persisting uncertainty and controversy are clear enough. What is at best a subordinate principle of
order within the state must be something altogether different within
a society that does not afford the measure of security normally
afforded to individuals within the state. Given the conditions that
have always characterized international society, it can hardly be
expected that here the scope of the right of self-defense will be as
narrowly defined or that the actual exercise of this right will be as
severely controlled as within the state. Moreover, to the extent that
the circumstances in which states may employ force generally as a
measure of self-help are progressively restricted—if this progressive
restriction is not accompanied by parallel change in the basic structural characteristics of international society—the significance attached
to the right of self-defense must if anything increase. Force may be
in principle forbidden to states, not only as a means for effecting
change but as a means for the protection of established rights. At the
same time, no viable and effective alternative to the institution of
self-help may exist.[7] In these circumstances, the scope of the right of
self-defense may largely determine the degree of security states enjoy,
since a right of self-redress that nevertheless forbids the threat or
use of force may prove insufficient to the task of preserving many of
the rights on which the security of the state rests.

These considerations largely explain the controversies that have
always attended interpretations of the critical provisions of the United
Nations Charter, controversies that find an echo in the disparate
interpretations of self-defense in current versions of *bellum justum*.

---

[7] The argument is no doubt true that the persistence of the institution of
self-help must impede progress toward an effectively centralized juridical organization of international society. It is no less true, however, that the absence of
such juridical organization must account for the persistence of states in retaining
the right of self-help. Unfortunately, these truisms do not carry us very far.

A restrictive view of the Charter's provisions, in limiting the right to exercise force in self-defense to the sole contingency of a prior armed attack, is vulnerable to the criticism that, if adhered to, it might well result in defeating the essential purpose of this right.[8] To require that an armed attack must have actually begun before the right of self-defense may be exercised is to exceed even the requirements for exercising self-defense imposed by most municipal legal systems which permit acts in self-defense not only against on actual danger but also against one that is imminent. The restrictive view would therefore appear to place more rigid requirements on the right of self-defense precisely in those circumstances where this right must continue to afford the principal basis for security. More generally, however, the objection to the restrictive view is simply that a state may be unable to preserve its vital interests—above all its political independence— if self-defense is only legitimate where the measures taken to endanger the state's interests take the form of an armed attack. The measures that may jeopardize a state's independence need not involve armed force, though they may nevertheless be unlawful. To deny states the right to respond to such measures by employing, if necessary, forcible measures in self-defense may well result in turning the right of political independence into little more than a sham. Nor is it useful here to draw a parallel between the state and international society. Within the state a right of self-defense is denied the individual short of an armed attack or the imminent threat of armed attack precisely because the individual may seek and receive protection against other acts endangering his vital and legally protected interests. The same assurance evidently does not obtain for states in international society. To require of states what is required of individuals within the state is to ignore the disparate circumstances that make the employment of armed force a reasonable condition for the exercise of self-defense in the one case and an unreasonable condition in the other case.

---

[8] Even the restrictive view, however, would leave a substantial measure of uncertainty over the permitted scope of self-defense. In limiting the right to exercise force in self-defense to the sole contingency of an armed attack, it is still necessary to determine what constitutes an armed attack. Need an armed attack be "direct" before it may be responded to with forcible measures of self-defense? Those who respond affirmatively cannot rely upon the United Nations Charter, since Article 51 of the Charter does not require that an armed attack be "direct" before it may be responded to with force. It may of course be argued that the consequence of including indirect uses of armed force within the concept of armed attack is to expand this concept to a point where it may well become meaningless as a restraint. This may be true. Yet it is also true that a state's independence may be jeopardized by the indirect employment of armed force.

Although this criticism of the restrictive view of the right of self-defense is not without considerable merit, it is much easier to make than to suggest an alternative that is not equally vulnerable to criticism. However paradoxical the restrictive view appears in denying the legitimacy of anticipatory acts of self-defense, the explanation of this apparent paradox must be found in those very conditions that normally attend the exercise of self-defense in international society. The same conditions that do indeed lend support to the argument on behalf of anticipatory acts of self-defense also point to the considerable dangers of granting such a right. Nor does the nature of modern weapons substantially alter this conclusion. If the speed and destructive power of modern weapons may defeat the purpose of self-defense in the absence of a right to take anticipatory measures against an imminent attack, it is these same characteristics of modern weapons that must also render a right to take anticipatory measures particularly dangerous and subject to abuse.

Apart from the issue of anticipatory self-defense, if the restrictive view of the right of self-defense is considered inadequate and unacceptable, what is the alternative? The broad response given this question has been to insist that the resort to forcible measures of self-defense is legitimate not only to protect the state's territorial integrity, its "physical person" against armed attack; self-defense is equally legitimate when resorted to for the protection of those interests which collectively comprise the state's "existence" in the broader sense of political independence and which may be endangered by measures other than armed force. But if uncertainty has always prevailed with respect to the scope of the rights—the legally protected interests—that presumably comprise the state's security and independence, an equal uncertainty must prevail with respect to the scope of the right of self-defense. Given the congenital disposition of states to interpret their existence, and threats thereto, expansively, the claim of self-defense, even when limited to the protection of legal rights against delictual conduct, may come very close in practice to the more general claim of a right of self-help.[9]

---

[9] There is the further consideration that a state's independence may be impaired by acts that do not involve the threat or use of armed force. To the extent that unlawful intervention is held to encompass only those acts of interference in the affairs of another state that take an imperative or dictatorial form and involve the threat or use of force, the duty of non-intervention becomes irrelevant in dealing with behavior that may nevertheless effectively jeopardize political independence. If the right of political independence is held to justify the resort to forcible measures of self-defense, and if the right of independence

The immediately preceding considerations have assumed that, however ill-defined in their scope, the acts in response to which self-defense is presumably legitimate are at least clearly unlawful. Measures of self-defense are permitted, then, in response to unlawful acts which, at the same time, endanger another state's territorial integrity or political independence. It is clear, however, that a state's political independence, and the security on which independence rests, may be endangered by acts which are not forbidden—at least, not specifically forbidden—by international law. In recent years, the most dramatic illustration of this possibility resulted from the discovery in October, 1962, that the Soviet Union was secretly establishing missile sites on the island of Cuba. The action of the Soviet Government was interpreted by the United States, as well as by the Organization of American States, to constitute a threat to the peace and security—and accordingly, the political independence—of the states comprising the Western Hemisphere, thereby justifying the resort to forcible measures designed to prevent the further shipment to Cuba of missiles and aircraft having an offensive capability as well as to compel the withdrawal of such weapons as were already on the island. Yet in sending these weapons the Soviet Government acted with the consent and cooperation of the Cuban Government. There is no rule of international law that specifically forbids a state from giving arms to another state or from establishing military bases in the territory of another state, whether openly or in a clandestine manner, so long as this is done with the latter state's consent. Nor does international law forbid a state from attempting to alter the military balance of power in its favor, so long as this is done through actions which do not in themselves violate the rights of other states. To the extent that the forcible measures taken by the United States in response to the action of the Soviet Government are nevertheless justified as measures of legitimate self-defense, they afford a striking example of the claim to take measures of self-defense against acts which are not at least *prima facie* unlawful.[10]

---

is only given a sufficiently broad interpretation, the result must be to enlarge the scope of self-defense to a point where it is difficult to distinguish from the much more general claim of the state to possess the competence to take measures of self-help—including forcible measures of self-help—as a reaction to acts of other states which violate its rights. These considerations explain, in part, why the claim of self-defense in the customary law always bordered in practice on the much more general claim of a right to self-help.

[10] In undertaking the naval quarantine of Cuba, however, the United States did not attempt to justify the action as a legitimate measure of self-defense. Nor

It may of course be argued that acts which endanger the security and independence of other states are unlawful even though they are not specifically forbidden by international law. This is, it would appear, the implication of the claim that a state has the right to take forcible measures of self-defense, if necessary, against any and all acts which endanger its political independence. But if this argument is once granted, it is not easy to see wherein it differs from the traditional claim of a right to self-preservation, a claim the meta-legal character of which has always been practically indistinguishable from the classic plea of necessity. If the substantive rights in defense of which force may be employed remain both expansive and ill-defined, if all that can be said with assurance is that in some vague manner these rights encompass the security and independence of the state, it is not easy to see wherein the right of self-defense limits the "necessities" of the state.[11]

---

did the Organization of American States attempt to characterize the Soviet action as one giving rise to a right of individual and collective self-defense.

[11] Thus the authors of a recent study point out that claims of self-defense "are claims to exercise highly intense coercion in response to what is alleged to be unlawfully initiated coercion." Myres S. McDougal and Florentino P. Feliciano, *Law and Minimum World Public Order* (1961), p. 209. The legally protected interests for the protection of which measures of self-defense may be undertaken are summarized as "territorial integrity and political independence." Political independence is defined as that "freedom of decision-making or self-direction customarily demanded by state officials. Impairment of 'political independence,' as an attack upon the institutional arrangements of authority and control in the target state, thus involves substantial curtailment of the freedom of decision-making through the effective and drastic reduction of the number of alternative policies open at tolerable costs to the officials of that state" (p. 177). On this view, measures of self-defense are legitimate in response to acts of coercion by another state which impair or threaten to impair this "freedom of decision-making" of the target state, provided only that such measures are necessary in the circumstances and proportionate to the danger. Nor is it necessary that the acts in response to which measures of self-defense are undertaken be specifically forbidden by international law. They are unlawful, on this view, if only their effect is to endanger a state's political independence. It is difficult to see any substantial difference between this view of self-defense and the older—and avowedly political —doctrine of self-preservation. Professor McDougal confirms this conclusion, without admitting it, in his remarks on the Cuban quarantine. Cf. Myres S. McDougal, "The Soviet-Cuban Quarantine and Self-Defense," 57 *American Journal of International Law* (July, 1963), 597ff. For a candid reaffirmation of the right of self-preservation in the context of the Cuban quarantine it is necessary to turn from the international jurists to a former Secretary of State, who declares: "I must conclude that the propriety of the Cuban quarantine is not a legal issue. The power, position and prestige of the United States had been challenged by another state and law simply does not deal with such questions of ultimate power—power

These uncertainties marking the scope of self-defense in international law are equally apparent in current versions of *bellum justum*. They are scarcely overcome by other restraints placed on the exercise of self-defense. The lawful exercise of force in self-defense presumably requires that the danger giving rise to this right be immediate and of such a nature as to leave no reasonable possibility for recourse to alternative means of protection. Even then, the use of force in self-defense must prove reasonable, and it may prove reasonable only if it is proportionate to the end of protecting those interests that are endangered. Force in excess of this purpose is forbidden, since action taken in self-defense is held to have a strictly preventive character.

It is clear that these requirements of law still leave largely unaffected the vital issue of the rights on behalf of which, and the acts in response to which, forcible measures of self-defense may be undertaken. Even so, the interpretation to be given these requirements has never been free from substantial uncertainty. Thus it has never been clear whether the requirement of proportionality limits acts taken in self-defense to repelling the immediate danger or permits action directed to removing the danger. The latter interpretation is not unreasonable, given the circumstances attending the exercise of self-defense in international society. Within domestic societies the state assures that a danger once repelled will be removed. Hence the justification for the severe restriction of measures taken in self-defense. In international society this assurance evidently cannot be given to states. Hence an equally severe restriction of measures taken in self-defense may prove unreasonable in that it may defeat the essential purpose for which measures of self-defense are permitted in the first place. The argument is not without merit. Yet if it is once accepted, it must become increasingly difficult to set meaningful limits to the exercise of self-defense.[12]

---

that comes close to the sources of sovereignty. . . . No law can destroy the state creating the law. The survival of states is not a matter of law." Remarks by the Hon. Dean Acheson, Proceedings, *American Society of International Law* (1963), p. 14.

[12] The issue of proportionality arose in the Suez crisis of 1956. In attacking Egypt, Israel justified her action as a legitimate measure of self-defense, taken in response to a continuous series of armed raids on Israeli territory by fedayeen bands based in Egypt and in anticipation of what was alleged to be an impending attack on Israel by Egyptian forces. Quite apart from the issue of anticipatory self-defense raised by the Israeli action, the obvious and acknowledged intent of the Israeli action was to destroy the fedayeen bases in Egypt, that is, to remove this particular source of danger. At the time, the action was generally condemned,

In substance, the same requirements of necessity and proportionality are also held to govern the just exercise of force. In *bellum justum*, it is true, the requirement of proportionality possesses a broader meaning than does the requirement of proportionality in international law. In the latter, the proportionality required is little more than what may be termed proportionality of effectiveness. In the former, the proportionality required is both a proportionality of effectiveness and a proportionality of value. In *bellum justum* it is not enough that the use of force is proportionate, though no more than proportionate, to the effective protection of endangered interests or values. To this proportionality of effectiveness must be added a proportionality of value, requiring that the values preserved through force are proportionate to the values sacrificed through force. Indeed, if anything, it is the proportionality of value rather than of effectiveness upon which primary emphasis is placed in *bellum justum*. At the same time, the requirement of a proportionality of value can hardly be regarded as a very meaningful restraint, however great the emphasis placed on it. Devoid entirely of the element of specificity, it is a prescription that can readily be adjusted to the most varied of actions. It is not surprising that the requirement of a proportionality of value has been invoked with an apparent plausibility on all sides of the nuclear issue by Christian moralists. It illustrates that a prescription the converse of which is manifestly absurd can tell us very little that is meaningful about how men ought to behave.[13]

---

among other reasons, because it was considered disproportionate and unreasonable to the acts provoking the Israeli attack. In defense of the Israeli position, however, it may be contended that the action was without purpose or reason unless directed to removing this source of danger. In this respect, it is interesting to compare the position taken by Israel in 1956 and the position taken by the United States in the Cuban crisis in 1962. Much has been made of the proportionality and reasonableness of the Cuban "quarantine" in view of the considerable danger allegedly posed by the presence of Soviet missile bases in Cuba. It should be noted, however, that the declared policy of the American government was not only to stop the further shipment of missiles to Cuba but to compel the withdrawal of such weapons as were already on the island, and to do so by any and all means that might prove necessary. The proportionality and reasonableness of the American position can hardly be judged exclusively in terms of the measures that were actually taken; it must also be judged in terms of the measures threatened if the quarantine proved ineffective and the missiles were not removed.

[13] It must be emphasized that the principle of proportionality (of value) does not of itself confer a distinctive quality on *bellum justum*. This principle is implicit in almost every conceivable justification of force. Not only does it express what may be termed the "logic of justification," it is compatible with almost every justification—or condemnation—of force men have ever given. It is frequently

The Means of War; Do Limits Exist?

If we are to find a distinctive quality in *bellum justum*, a quality that sets clear and meaningful limits to the necessities of the state, that quality simply cannot be found in the causes and ends of war. Nor can it be found in the general principles governing the conditions of war. If this quality is to be found at all, it must instead be found in the restraints placed on the conduct or means of war. To say this is not to imply that the doctrine of *bellum justum*, whether in its classic or in its modern versions, has indeed made the means of warfare the center of moral gravity.[14] On the contrary, it is in the

---

assumed that the difficulty in applying the principle of proportionality, and the limited utility of the principle when it is applied, result from men's inability to know all the facts of a situation and, above all, from men's inability to foresee the consequences of their actions. This is certainly true, but it is by no means the whole truth. Even if all the relevant facts were known, and all of the consequences of action (or abstention from action) foreseen, the application of the principle of proportionality would give rise to uncertainty and, in consequence, to disagreement. This is so for the apparent reason that the principle of proportionality is devoid of substantive content. The principle of proportionality prescribes that the good resulting from the use of force ought to outweigh, or to be proportionate to, the evil attending force. This is merely an elaborate way of saying not only what is evidently implied in the very task of justifying force but what all men can readily agree upon. There is no real consensus, however, among theorists of the just war with respect to the values that should form the content of the principle of proportionality. To be sure, there is agreement that the state, though it is considered an important value, cannot be considered the supreme value. Hence, the application of the principle of proportionality by theorists of *bellum justum* may lead to results that are different from the results of applying this principle by those who impute supreme value to the state and, accordingly, to the state's necessities. But this difference is scarcely sufficient to establish a meaningful consensus among the former with respect to the values that should form the content of the principle of proportionality. Moreover, even if we assume that men can know all of the consequences of their actions and can achieve meaningful agreement on the plurality of values the preservation of which may justify war, there is still no objective way of determining (calculating) whether the evil attendant upon the waging of war is justified in terms of the good obtained through war; reasonable men can, and will, reach quite disparate conclusions. Of course, the requirement of proportionality would give a distinctive character to *bellum justum* if it afforded a distinctive method of determining (calculating) a proportionality of value and one that somehow avoided these difficulties. This is admittedly not the case. The scales used by the theorists of the just war are the same scales used by others (though the weights are presumably different), and the results are quite as uncertain and subject to controversy. With respect to the manner of establishing either proportionality or disproportionality in war, then, there is little, if indeed anything, that is distinctive in *bellum justum*.

[14] Whether the theory of the just war *should* always have made the conduct of war the center of moral gravity is another matter. In this connection Paul

19

causes and ends justifying war that we must find the principal focus of the doctrine. It is true that in many contemporary analyses of the just war the means permitted in war have been given markedly increased attention. Even so, it would be rash to conclude that at present primary emphasis is placed on the manner in which war must be conducted. In this respect, as in many others, the evolution of *bellum justum* appears to parallel the evolution of international law. In both, it is the *jus ad bellum,* or, perhaps more accurately, a *jus contra bellum,* rather than a *jus in bello* that has formed the primary emphasis. Moreover, to the extent that the manner of warfare

---

Ramsey has written: "Since at least everyone seeks peace and desires justice, the ends for which war may legitimately be fought are not nearly so important in the theory of the just war as is the moral and political wisdom contained in its reflection upon the conduct or means of warfare. Unless there is a morality applicable to instruments of war and intrinsically limiting its conduct, then we must simply admit that war has no limits—since these can hardly be derived from 'peace' as the 'final cause' of just wars." "The case for making 'just war' possible," John C. Bennett, ed., *Nuclear Weapons and the Conflict of Conscience* (1962), pp. 146–147. Although Ramsey's latter assertion is an exaggeration, neglecting as it does the moderating effects limited ends in war may have on the conduct of war, even if it were accepted as true it would not follow that his former assertion must also be true. Nor can imaginative reconstructions of the *bellum justum* doctrine, such as Ramsey's (cf. *War and the Christian Conscience*), prove more than what the theory of the just war should perhaps have always had as its central emphasis, given the premises from which it starts. In fact, it is surprising how little emphasis was placed on the means of warfare by expositors of the traditional doctrine. It is this relative neglect along with the emphasis placed on the interpretation of war as an act of vindicative justice undertaken for the punishment of the wicked that has prompted critics to conclude that far from leading to greater restraint in the conduct of war the traditional doctrine had the contrary effect. Whatever the merit of this criticism, it is a matter of record that the greatest progress in the mitigation of war came in a period when the idea of the just war was in eclipse. No doubt, this progress cannot be attributed simply to the decline of *bellum justum.* Other and more important factors were at work in the eighteenth and nineteenth centuries which explain the limited wars of the period and the growing observance in war of the immunity of the civilian population. Even so, a persuasive case may be made for the position that the interpretation of war as a duel between equals significantly contributed to the humanization of warfare. There are perhaps no logical reasons why the interpretation of war as a duel between equals, rather than as the punishment of the wicked, should lead to greater restraint in the conduct of war, but there are very persuasive psychological reasons which suggest this result. These reasons are scarcely offset by the claim that the wicked are to be punished for love's sake, for the sake of a love that comprises the enemy but at the same time does not preclude—in St. Augustine's words—"a benevolent severity." For all his realism, Augustine's insistence upon the loving killer, or the loving avenger, who would vindicate justice though without passion and self assertion was not very realistic.

20

has been increasingly emphasized, the significance of this emphasis must largely be seen in the effects it has had in redefining the *jus ad bellum*.[15]

Despite these considerations, it is over the issue of the means permitted in war, or to deter war, that we must find, if anywhere, a significant conflict between the necessities of the state and the demands of *bellum justum*. The general nature that conflict must take is clear enough. Whereas reason of state must reject the claim that there are any inherent limits on the means that may be threatened or employed to preserve the state, *bellum justum* must insist that there are such limits and that whatever the circumstances they may never be transgressed.[16] The argument of necessity must reject the claim of inherent limits on the means of war not because it is informed by an "ethic of responsibility" and therefore requires the statesman to calculate and to weigh the possible consequences of alternative courses of action, but because it presupposes as an ultimate end the preservation and continuity of the state. The doctrine of *bellum justum* evidently cannot share this presupposition else it could not insist that there are means that may never be employed. At the same time, there is no denial here of the need to calculate and to weigh possible consequences of alternative courses of action. There is simply the insistence that whatever the results of calculation, certain limits must be imposed on the means permitted the statesman, limits that may never be transgressed.[17]

------

[15] That is, in restricting the circumstances or occasions in which the resort to armed force is considered justified.

[16] It must be made clear that this conflict is not over the proportionality or disproportionality of means, in terms of their effects, but over the means themselves. The distinction is a critical one, since it is not only over the issue of means, *per se*, that a clear conflict may arise between reason of state and *bellum justum*.

[17] The position taken in the text is at variance with what is perhaps the prevailing view of this conflict, a view that reflects the position taken by Max Weber in his now classic essay "Politics as a Vocation" (cf. *From Max Weber: Essays in Sociology*, H. H. Gerth and C. Wright Mills (1948), pp. 77ff.). In this essay Weber wrote: "We must be clear about the fact that all ethically oriented conduct may be guided by two fundamentally differing and irreconcilably opposed maxims: conduct can be oriented to an 'ethic of ultimate ends' or to an 'ethic of responsibility.' This is not to say that an ethic of ultimate ends is identical with irresponsibility, or that an ethic of responsibility is identical with unprincipled opportunism. Naturally nobody says that. However, there is an abysmal contrast between conduct that follows the maxim of an ethic of ultimate ends—that is, in religious terms, 'The Christian does rightly and leaves the result with the Lord'— and conduct that follows the maxim of an ethic of responsibility, in which case one has to give an account of the foreseeable results of one's actions." In con-

To the degree that *bellum justum* has a distinctive quality, then, this quality is to be found not merely in the significance given to the means of action but above all in the insistence that *bellum justum* is an "ethic of ultimate means." This quality is blurred, if not lost, if the problem of means is itself reduced to what is, in effect, another form of calculation. Thus it is not enough to argue that one may never do evil that good may come because the good will not come (only the evil), or that the evil act will corrupt the actor and thereby defeat his ends (however desirable in themselves), or that the means cannot be separated from the ends but are themselves the ends in the very process of coming into existence. It is not enough to argue in this manner if only for the reason that each of these familiar contentions is open to question. Whether the use of evil means will always and necessarily defeat the ends of action, if only by corrupting the actor, is not an issue that can be decided in the abstract. No doubt, the task of the moralist would be greatly simplified if it could be so decided. He would then enjoy the best of both worlds. If certain means are never to be employed, or threatened, it is not only because they are in and of themselves evil but also because they are, after all, imprudent, a mistaken form of calculation. Unfortunately, experience shows that good may come of evil, that the use of evil means does not always corrupt the actor and that it is much too simple to conceive of means as themselves the ends of action in the very process of coming into existence.[18] If certain means are to be absolutely forbidden

trasting an "ethic of responsibility" with an "ethic of ultimate ends," Weber presumably implies that an ethic of responsibility is *not* an ethic of ultimate ends. But this is not true—at any rate, it is not necessarily true. The statesman has as his highest moral imperative the preservation of the state entrusted to his care. If we say that he must act responsibly we mean that he must take all possible care to estimate the results or consequences of his actions. In saying this, however, we do not mean that the statesman has no ultimate end. Although the statesman must act prudently in preserving the state entrusted to his care, he must nevertheless preserve the state whatever the means. We might just as well say then that Weber's ethic of responsibility is an ethic of ultimate ends precisely because the statesman must—if necessary—subordinate the means to the ends of action. On the other hand, we might just as accurately call Weber's ethic of ultimate ends an "ethic of ultimate means." The statement that the Christian does rightly and leaves the results with the Lord means, if anything, that certain acts (means) are never to be employed whatever the consequences that may follow from their non-employment. The Christian does not feel "irresponsible" for the consequences any more than the statesmen feels "irresponsible" for the means. It is simply a question whether one accepts absolute restraints on action, whatever the ends sought, or whether one does not do so.

[18] Were the means employed by the Allies in World War II little more than the ends of action in the very process of coming into existence? Did they corrupt,

they must be forbidden quite apart from these considerations. If certain means are to be absolutely forbidden they must be so forbidden because of their intrinsic evil. If one may never do evil that good may come, it is not—or not primarily—because the good probably will not come but simply because one may never do evil.

Taken by itself, however, the bare assertion that there are absolute restraints on the means permitted even in war does not tell us what it is that is absolutely forbidden. Nor are we appreciably enlightened with respect to that conduct absolutely forbidden when we are further told that we may never do evil, or threaten to do evil, that good may come. If evil signifies that which is absolutely forbidden, we have simply been told what we already knew or should have known; that which is absolutely forbidden is evidently that which may never be done. The position that certain means may never be employed, or threatened, even to preserve the independence and continuity of the state does clearly mean that the state cannot be considered a supreme value for men. Moreover, if the survival of the state cannot serve to justify certain means, it follows that those values the state, and perhaps only the state, may serve to protect also cannot be considered supreme. But these conclusions, however significant they may be, still do not afford us much guidance with respect to that conduct which is absolutely forbidden.

It is another matter to identify the one restraint that in some form must be observed in war if this activity is to prove amenable to substantive limitation. Apart from the limitation the ends of war may impose on the conduct of war, it is apparent that this conduct can be significantly limited only by limiting those individuals who may be

---

as presumably they invariably must corrupt, the actors? It requires a very perverse reading of contemporary history to answer these questions affirmatively. Yet there are many Christian moralists who continue to insist that these questions must be answered affirmatively. To say this is not of course to justify the means employed in World War II. It is simply to say that the moralist who condemns certain means as intrinsically evil cannot expect to support his argument on every occasion by absolutizing what are in reality no more than prudential maxims. The temptation to do just this, however, is very great. Thus in recent years the condemnation by Christian moralists of policies of deterrence has often proceeded not only, and not even primarily, from the position that such policies imply the intent to do evil, and are accordingly to be considered in the same proscribed category as the doing of evil, but from the position that they are ultimately a form of bad calculation (i.e., either that they will issue in catastrophic conflict, or that they will corrupt the actors even if they do not issue in such conflict, etc.). As the age of deterrence progresses, the latter argument becomes less and less persuasive, even, one suspects, for those who advance it.

made the objects of attack. It is equally apparent that the only basis of the distinction to be drawn between those who may be made the objects of attack and those who may not be so made must rest upon the degree of involvement or participation in warlike activities. Historically, the importance of this distinction for the law of war is generally acknowledged. The development of a body of rules regulating, and limiting, the conduct of war has been largely synonymous with the development of the principle distinguishing between the armed forces (combatants) and the civilian population (noncombatants) of belligerents, and requiring belligerents both to refrain from making the civilian population the deliberate object of attack and to safeguard this population from injuries not incidental to operations undertaken against combatant forces and other legitimate military objectives. The decline in this century of the practices traditionally regulating the manner of warfare has also been largely synonymous with the decline of this principle.

It is the same principle that forms the main limitation on the just conduct of war. In the doctrine of *bellum justum,* however, the norm forbidding the direct and intentional attack on noncombatants represents an absolute injunction. At any rate, it is only with those versions of *bellum justum* which do so regard this norm that we are here concerned. For it is only where the prohibition against the deliberate killing of noncombatants is considered absolute that a clear conflict may arise between the necessities of the state and the requirements of an ethic which presumably sets limits to these necessities. In the theory of the just war the distinction in question is held to define the essential difference between war and murder; that is, the essential difference between the permitted and the forbidden taking of human life. It is the deliberate killing of the innocent that is always to be avoided, that may never be justified even as a reprisal measure taken in response to similar measures of an adversary. This is, in substance, the evil that may never be done, or threatened, that good may come.

Despite the absolute character given it, whether, and to what extent, the norm forbidding the direct and intentional attack upon the innocent does set significant limits to the necessities of the state are not self-answering questions. Restraints may be absolute in character yet innocuous in terms of the specific behavior they are interpreted to forbid. In forbidding the deliberate attack upon the innocent we must still determine who are the innocent and what constitutes a deliberate attack upon them. The answer to the first question does not present considerable difficulties provided only that the innocent are equated with noncombatants and the latter identified—as, indeed, they have been traditionally identified—by the remoteness of their relationship to warlike activities. Difficulties may of course arise, and persist, over the precise characteristics requisite for noncombatant status, but unless the very concept of noncombatant status is itself suppressed these difficulties are not likely to prove intractable.[19] The answer to the second question does pose very considerable difficulties, however, and it can scarcely be said that these difficulties have been any more satisfactorily resolved by theorists of *bellum justum* than by international jurists. That the former attribute an absolute character to the norm forbidding the direct and intentional attack upon the innocent only serves to accentuate rather than to resolve these difficulties.

In the practice of states the principle distinguishing between combatants and noncombatants has never been interpreted as giving the latter complete protection from the hazards of war. It has always been accepted that if war is to prove at all possible the immunity of noncombatants must be qualified, and substantially so. Thus the investment, bombardment, siege and assault of fortified places, including towns and cities, have always been recognized as legitimate meas-

---

[19] Even so, these difficulties do at least indicate that the absolute prohibition against attacking the innocent rests on a distinction that is far more relative and pragmatic in application than is commonly admitted. Theorists of *bellum justum* regularly point out that the concept of "innocence" corresponds to the concept of "noncombatancy" and, indeed, use these presumably coresponding terms interchangeably. In state practice, however, the distinction drawn between combatants and noncombatants has always had a relative character, in the sense that at the very least its application has been dependent both on the manner in which states organize for war and on the technology with which they conduct war. To this extent, then, it has always been true that the scope of noncombatancy could vary, and has varied, considerably; hence the scope of innocence could also vary, and has varied, considerably. Moreover, the relative character of the concept of noncombatant status is unavoidably a function as well of the degree of remoteness from warlike activities that is held to constitute this status. It is no doubt true that if the concept of noncombatant status is to be granted in principle, remoteness from warlike activities cannot be pushed beyond certain limits. Yet it must be admitted that what these limits are in practice is an issue over which reasonable men may differ and have frequently differed. Theorists of *bellum justum* sometimes assume that because the concept of innocence, like the concept of noncombatancy, depends upon objective behavior and not a subjective state of mind (i.e., personal innocence or guilt) that this concept is thereby susceptible to objective determination. But this is not true. Though the status of noncombatants, as well as the status of innocents, depends on objective behavior, the determination of either depends on a subjective appreciation of this behavior. In the subjective interpretation of this behavior there is no apparent reason for according greater weight to the insights of Christian moralists than to the insights of others.

ures of warfare, even though such places may contain large numbers of peaceful inhabitants. More generally, belligerents have never been required to cease military operations because of the presence of noncombatants within the immediate area of these operations or to refrain from attacking military objectives simply because of the proximity of military objectives to the noncombatant population. These qualifications to the principle of noncombatant immunity are to be explained in terms of military necessity, which permits belligerents to take those measures required for the success of military operations and not otherwise forbidden by the law of war (in this instance, not forbidden by some rule other than the principle distinguishing between combatants and noncombatants). To this extent, then, the scope afforded to the principle of noncombatant immunity has always been dependent upon the scope afforded to military necessity.

The same dependence upon military necessity is apparent in considering the concept of military objective. Time and again the attempt has been made to limit the concept of military objective by freeing it from the uncertainty and potential expansiveness of military necessity. Time and again the attempt has failed and has served only to emphasize the dependence in practice of the meaning given to military objective on the meaning given to military necessity. The essentially indeterminate character of the concept of military objective therefore reflects the essentially indeterminate character of the concept of military necessity, dependent as the latter is in any given period upon the manner in which societies organize for and conduct war, the technology with which war is waged and the ends for which war is undertaken. No doubt, it is true that if the principle of noncombatant immunity is to be retained at all in war there must be *some* limits placed on this relationship of dependency. Whatever the meaning given to military necessity, noncombatants cannot as such be considered a military objective. But short of the clear negation of the principle of noncombatant immunity, what these limits must be in practice has never been clear. All that can be said with assurance— all that could ever be said with assurance—is only that the scope of the immunity accorded the civilian population is largely dependent upon the meaning given to the concept of military objective and that the concept of military objective varies as the character of war—hence the character of military necessity—varies. Moreover, even if it were possible to resolve the uncertainty that marks the concept of military objective there would still remain the problem of determining the extent of the incidental or indirect injury that may be inflicted upon the civilian population in the course of attacking military objectives.

The answer to this latter problem, however, remains as uncertain and controverted as does the answer to the problem of what constitutes a legitimate military objective. To the extent the attempt has been made to answer it, the basis of that attempt has largely been through recourse to the very principle—military necessity—that accounts for the uncertainty attending the scope of military objective and that, in consequence, gave rise to the problem in the first place.

The general import of these considerations is clear enough. However critical the principle distinguishing between combatants and noncombatants may be for the regulation and limitation of war, this principle has always had a relative and contingent character in state practice as well as in the law that emerged from this practice. As such, the scope afforded it has always been subject to the imperious claims of necessity, the manifestations of which in the conduct of war are to be found in the claims of military necessity and of reprisal. Indeed, so pervasive is this subjection that belligerents have been able in practice to reduce the effective scope of the principle of noncombatant immunity almost to a vanishing point while nevertheless affirming the continued validity of this principle. Even where the attack upon noncombatants is openly avowed as direct and intentional, the continued affirmation of the principle of noncombatant immunity may be given a semblance of plausibility if the action is represented as a reprisal taken in response to similar behavior of an adversary.

In giving the principle of noncombatant immunity an absolute and unconditioned character, the doctrine of *bellum justum* presumably rejects this subordination to the claims of necessity. Since it may clearly do so only at a very high price, however, the temptation is understandably great to pose a rejection which, in terms of the specific consequences that may be drawn from it (hence the practical limits it imposes on military necessity), is more apparent than real. If *bellum justum* requires that the innocent may never be made the deliberate object of attack, the question nevertheless remains in what circumstances this absolute prohibition is deemed to have been transgressed. In answering this question the theorists of the just war have very little to say that is distinctive or instructive with respect to what constitutes a legitimate military objective. Apart from being told what we already knew, that noncombatants cannot as such be considered a legitimate military objective, we are left in quite as uncertain a position as before over what does constitute a legitimate military objective. Moreover, it must be made clear that no more than international law does *bellum justum* require a belligerent to refrain from attacking military objectives simply because of the proximity of these objectives to the civilian population. What *bellum justum* does require is that in attacking military objectives the death and injury done to noncombatants be beside the intention—at any rate, beside the direct or positive intention—of the attacker, that this death and injury done to noncombatants not constitute a means for achieving an otherwise legitimate military end and that, finally, the evil effect of the action not prove disproportionate to the good—or, at any rate, the morally sanctioned—effect.[20]

These requirements constitute the essential contribution of *bellum justum* to the vital issue of means. That they fail to provide a clear let alone a satisfactory solution to this vital issue is perhaps less a criticism of them than a testimony to the intractibility of the issue to which they are addressed. Nor is it the essential indeterminacy of intent that compels this conclusion, since *bellum justum* plainly requires more than subjective intention in judging the quality of action. Not only does it emphasize along with intent the objective consequences of action, for the most part it deduces intent from these consequences. Whether or not the actor is deemed to have intended to do evil is determined, in the absence of acknowledged intent to do evil, by inquiry into the character of the means he has chosen. The character of the means he has chosen is in turn determined

---

[20] The general principle involved here, and which comprises the above conditions, is commonly termed the principle of double effect. There are some variations in the formulation of these conditions. Thus it is often said that of the two effects of a permitted action, the first, and good effect is directly or positively intended while the second, and evil effect must be beside the actor's intention or only indirectly intended. In any event, the evil effect cannot be a means to the good effect. Hence, in the chain of consequences or in the order of causality—though not necessarily in order of time—the good effect must either precede or be immediate with the evil effect, else the evil effect would presumably cause, or be a means to, the good. The principle of double effect therefore attempts to reconcile the injunction against doing evil that good may come with the taking of certain acts that are known, and even known with certainty, to entail evil effects. In the case of war it is evident that this attempted reconciliation is mandatory if war is to be sanctioned at all, since evil effects of varying magnitude—i.e., the death and injury of the innocent—form an unavoidable effect of war. Of the three conditions set out in the text only the first two are examined in succeeding pages. The third requirement, that of proportionality, has already been discussed in relation to the justice of war in general. The indeterminacy of this test in a narrower context is almost as great as it must prove to be in a broader context, even though some writers attempt to reduce this indeterminacy by insisting that the effects, both evil and good, must be the "immediate" effects. No useful purpose is served by raising once again those considerations brought forth in earlier pages. Even so, the extreme limits to which the test of proportionality has been pushed by some moralists is significant and will be noted in a later connection.

by inquiry into the action itself, above all by inquiry into the consequences following from or the consequences that might have been reasonably expected to follow from the action. Yet it is precisely this dependence on the objective—indeed, on the quantitative—character of action to which just war theorists are ultimately driven that lays bare the largely relative nature of the judgments they must make.[21] In practice, whether the death and injury done to the innocent is directly intended or is beside the intention of the actor is determined by the scope of this death and injury. But there are no objective criteria for determining how much death and injury may be done to the innocent while still preserving the right intention, or, conversely, when such death and injury must establish the wrong intention. In the absence of such criteria it is clear that the judgments men make will be influenced in varying degree, whether consciously or unconsciously, by the claims of necessity. What was apparently excluded at the front door is therefore admitted in large measure through the back door.

Nor is this all. The attempt to reconcile the necessities of war—of any war—with the injunction against doing evil that good may come can be undertaken only by virtue of an implausible, or, at any rate, an artificial, notion of means. If it is known with certainty that

---

[21] It is not enough to admit this dependence without drawing the full consequences from that admission. Thus Paul Ramsey writes: "It is the virtue, and perhaps the irrelevance, of modern formulations of the rule of double effect in the theory of the just war that, by requiring more than subjective intention, by requiring that objectively also the intrinsically evil effect of the slaying of innocent people be not a means to whatsoever military advantage, we are brought close to the rejection of all modern warfare." *War and the Christian Conscience*, p. 64. But how can we tell whether or not this slaying is a means rather than a second or indirect effect? Surely we cannot do so through analyzing intentions as such, since the indeterminacy of intent gave rise to the problem in the first place. Nor can we do so through study of the sequence or order of action. The second effect need not come later in time. Ramsey goes on to note: "It is a question of which effect is, in the objective order, incidental to which, even when both effects are produced at the same time from a single action." But this is clearly a matter of quantity then—of objective consequences. Another writer, discussing the principle of double effect in much the same terms as Ramsey, declares: "It is nonsense to pretend that you do not intend to do what is the means you take to your chosen end. Otherwise there is absolutely no substance to the Pauline teaching that we may not do evil that good may come." G. E. M. Anscombe, "War and Murder" in Walter Stein, ed., *Nuclear Weapons and Christian Conscience* (1961), p. 59. This statement leaves in abeyance the critical issue: what are the means you take to your chosen end? Are they determined by inquiry into the intention of the actor or by inquiry into the nature of the end the actor seeks and the character of the measures without which this end cannot be achieved?

in attacking a military objective death and injury will be inflicted upon the innocent, if it is known that two effects will follow inevitably from the action, the destruction of the military objective and the death and injury of noncombatants, is it still plausible to assert as theorists of *bellum justum* do assert that the one effect is a means while the other effect is not? Ordinarily, we regard a certain effect as a means to an end if that end cannot be secured without this effect, if the realization of the one is dependent, and is known to be dependent, upon the occurrence of the other. If this view is accepted, the death and injury inflicted on the innocent in the course of attacking a military objective is as much a means as is the destruction of the military objective. Whereas the one effect, destruction of the military objective, is a means to the end of victory in war, the other effect, the death and injury of noncombatants, is indirectly a means to the same end and directly a means to the end of destroying the military objective. Both effects, however, must be considered as means. It is true that one may avoid this conclusion, and thereby deny that the effect of inflicting death and injury on noncombatants is a means, by equating the notion of means with the question of intent. On this latter view, the one effect is a means because it is intended while the other effect, although it is foreseen, is not a means because it is presumably not intended, at least not directly intended, only reluctantly permitted. But this view not only must raise those difficulties attending the determination of intent considered above, it must also impute a meaning to intent that is very questionable. If it is known that an act will have certain evil consequences, and the act is nevertheless taken, it is plausible to contend that some of these consequences were not intended only if intent is made synonymous with wish or desire. This equation, however, accords neither with ordinary usage nor with common sense. We may not wish or desire something to happen, yet we may intend it to happen. The reason for this distinction is simply that to intend means to have in mind as something to be done or brought about. Thus we may not wish or desire a certain consequence of action and consider this consequence as tragic or as an evil. Even so, we intend this consequence if we know that it will result from a certain action and we nevertheless take this action.[22]

---

[22] There is a further point to be made in this connection. To say, as do the theorists of *bellum justum*, that an act must "positively intend only the good effect and merely tolerate the evil effect" is to give a moral significance to the notion of intent without resolving the real difficulty. Objectively, we still intend the one effect just as much as we intend the other effect. It does not alter matters to characterize the one effect as positively intended and the other effect as merely

It is altogether understandable that theorists of *bellum justum* have been so insistent upon tying an implausible notion of means to an equally implausible notion of intent, in view of the critical purpose this association serves. Once it is abandoned the attempt to reconcile the necessities of any war with the injunction that evil may not be done must also be abandoned. Yet to abandon this vain reconciliation is not also to abandon the position that means must remain limited; to acknowledge that it is not possible to wage war without doing evil is not thereby to open the door to any and every evil. There are still means and means, just as there is still evil and evil. If the issue that must be faced and somehow resolved is not whether one may do evil that good may come but rather how much evil one may do that any good may come, it is not for this reason without significance. There is surely a very important difference between the destruction of a city in order to destroy a military objective within or near the city and the destruction of the military objective, although destruction of the military objective inevitably involves inflicting some death and injury on noncombatants. There is still a very important difference even if we acknowledge that in both cases the death and injury done to the innocent is a means to the desired effect (end) and that in both cases this death and injury is intended. Whereas in the one case the death and injury done to noncombatants is, or may be, itself desired, in the other case it is not. If the one means is compatible with warfare that still retains significant limits, the other means is either not compatible or much less so. Above all, perhaps, is simply the difference in the objective consequences, the quantitative effects, of the two actions.

---

tolerated. Moreover, even the moral significance implied thereby is not without difficulty. When a military objective is attacked, death and suffering always result if only for combatants. De we "positively intend" this, is it a "good effect?" To the Christian moralist it would hardly seem so. From his point of view what we should "positively intend" is to repel injustice. The "good effect" is the repelling of injustice or perhaps the vindication of justice. The death and suffering inflicted on combatants is not as such a good effect. It too, is an evil that is tolerated, though only tolerated, in order to achieve a good end (effect). Of course, it is an evil that is far more tolerable than other evils, e.g. the death and suffering of noncombatants. Once again, the point must be stressed that at issue here is not whether one evil is greater than, or less tolerable than, the other evil but whether both evils (effects) must be considered as means. This issue cannot be resolved by endless, and inconclusive, discussion of the question of intent. Even if we were to concede that what is "indirectly intended," or "reluctantly permitted," is somehow different from what is "directly intended," or "positively permitted," it does not follow that the effect only indirectly intended is not a means. It too is a means, though it is a means that may be distinguished from the means that is directly intended or positively permitted.

There is no compelling reason, then, why we must accept the contention that if it is once accepted that evil must be done in war the issue of means is dissolved and any behavior sanctioned. This result *may* follow. The assumption that it *must* follow is no more compelling than the assumption that if men only believe that evil may never be done their behavior will thereby be restrained. Instead of restraining their behavior, the belief that evil may never be done may only strain their ingenuity. If evil may never be done, the practical significance of this injunction will still depend on the manner in which doing evil is conceived. Given sufficient ingenuity of conception, war takes on the character of an event in which ever greater evil effects may result yet apparently through no evil acts. In the most recent, and perhaps the most impressive, example of this ingenuity of conception it is argued that even the waging of a thermonuclear war need not imply the doing of evil so long as belligerents employ their weapons only against counterforce targets and other legitimate military objectives. The death and injury suffered by civilian populations would admittedly constitute a very great evil, but these evil effects might still be justified. At any rate, these evil effects, whatever might be said of their proportionality or disproportionality, would still not be the doing of evil. And if this use of nuclear weapons is not the doing of evil, it seems clearer still that the threat to use nuclear weapons against military objectives need not be considered forbidden.

Moreover, in order to remove lingering doubts about an intent to do evil, the threat to use nuclear weapons against military objectives may be attended by the express renunciation of an intent ever to use these weapons directly against a civilian population. In view of the magnitude of the expected destruction that would still be indirectly inflicted on the civilian population in the course of a direct attack on military objectives, deterrence would in all likelihood remain effective. Finally, however frequent and vehement the disclaimer of an intent directly to attack the civilian population of a potential adversary, even as a measure of reprisal in response to a similar attack, the character of nuclear weapons is such that an adversary can never be assured the weapons will not be used in this manner. This residual uncertainty results not only from the inherently ambiguous character of these weapons; it also, and perhaps more importantly, results from men's inability to predict with any real confidence what the consequences will be of using nuclear weapons and, indeed, whether their use can be reasonably controlled at all. This residual uncertainty forms the capstone of the deterrent system;

it cannot be removed from this system short of the dismantling of the system through destruction of the weapons themselves.[23]

It is roughly in this manner that the attempt has been made to bring both nuclear deterrence and even the waging of thermonuclear

---

[23] The position summarized above has been articulated at length by Paul Ramsey, *The Limits on Nuclear War* (1963) and "More Unsolicited Advice to Vatican Council II," in *Peace, The Churches and the Bomb* (1965). What makes Ramsey's writings of particular interest is not only the ingenuity with which he develops the argument for a just deterrent strategy and a just nuclear war strategy, should deterrence fail, but that he does so while remaining firmly committed to the more general position that the distinctive quality of *bellum justum* must be found in the restraints on the means of warfare, that there are certain means which because of their intrinsic evil may never be justifiably employed and that a largely teleological view of the Christian ethic, in refusing to place absolute limits on means, leads to the suspension—indeed, to the ultimate perversion—of an essential part of that ethic. This general position Ramsey set out in detail in his earlier study, *War and the Christian Conscience*. In the two later essays, cited above, he is concerned to show, first, that if war is to be a "rational politically purposive activity" it must be predominantly a "trial of strength" rather than a "test of resolve" or "battle of wills" and, second, that if war is so conceived it is possible to fashion a just—*and effective*—deterrent strategy as well as a just policy for waging nuclear war. Ramsey assumes that if war is a trial of strength it must thereby have limited means. If, however, war is a test of wills it must have essentially unlimited (and subjective) purposes; accordingly, it very probably must also be conducted by unlimited means. In terms of nuclear strategies, the former concept of war will go no higher than counterforce warfare whereas the latter concept may—and probably will—go to city exchanges (*The Limits on Nuclear War*, pp. 17–20). The argument is unpersuasive, however, because the essential distinction on which it rests is untenable. Will, or resolve, is a decisive ingredient in any "trial of strength." It is indeed difficult to imagine the character of a trial of strength that at the same time would not also be a trial of will or test of resolve. Of course, it is another matter to argue that the measures taken in war should be roughly commensurate or proportionate to the purposes of war, and, accordingly, that war *both* as a trial of strength and as a test of wills should reflect this commensurability. This counsel of perfection, which in practice men have seldom been able to meet, still says nothing about the nature of the purposes men should entertain in war. Instead, it merely says that whatever these purposes may be, the measures taken in war should be commensurate to them. Even so, one apparent qualification to this counsel is the sometimes advantageous tactic of attempting to obtain one's purposes either without a trial of strength altogether or with a minimum trial of strength by appearing more determined (resolved) than an opponent. If there are obvious limits to this tactic, they are very difficult to fix with any precision if only for the reason that the worth men set on the purposes or interests for which they fight and consequently the lengths to which they are prepared to go in order to obtain or to defend these purposes or interests, are difficult to fix with any precision. It is no adequate answer to this consideration to insert the antidote of common sense and to insist that some interests are still more

war into apparent conformity with the requirements on means laid down by *bellum justum*. The cumulative effect of that attempt is to reduce to a hollow shell the injunction against doing, or intending to do, evil that good may come. Not only does it strain the notion of

---

important than other interests, which is undoubtedly true, or that an opponent cannot be persuaded that all your interests are equally vital to you simply because you insist they are equally vital, which is also true. Despite these necessary, though obvious, limitations the fact remains that in most major conflicts there is a significant, and persistent, area of uncertainty in which one may obtain one's purposes by appearing more determined, and by being more determined, than an opponent. Moreover, there is the critically important consideration that the temptation to substitute a trial of wills for a trial of strength is roughly commensurate to the prospect of horrendous consequences issuing from a trial of strength. The relevance of this consideration in the case of almost any trial of strength between nuclear powers need not be labored. Indeed, to the extent that this prospect appears so horrendous as to render increasingly incommensurable the relation between the consequences of employing nuclear arms and the purposes or interests to be secured through such employment, to that extent the temptation, amounting almost to a compulsion, arises to substitute a trial of wills for what was heretofore a trial of strength and a trial of wills. In other terms, the trial of wills to which we give the name deterrence increasingly becomes the modern analogue of the wars of former periods; instead of "acting" out their conflicts, men are increasingly driven to "play" them out. In a nuclear age, then, the "spiritualization" of war appears inevitable unless nuclear powers are to abandon war altogether (i.e., in spirit and in form) in their mutual relations or to "conventionalize" nuclear wars. Ramsey's argument provides no persuasive considerations that the latter wars may prove feasible. Despite his sometimes all-too-confident statements about "limited counterforce warfare," his argument that just deterrent strategies are possible rests in part precisely on the uncertainty—indeed, the skepticism—that nuclear war can be so limited. Finally, in drawing his distinction between trials of strength and trials of wills, Ramsey neglects altogether the consideraiton that in any conflict, nuclear or otherwise, the importance of will depends upon the stakes of conflict. Thus in what is primarily a hegemonial conflict will becomes supremely important precisely because what is at stake is not whose will is to prevail in order to secure some other, and perhaps limited, objective but whose will is to prevail in order to prevail. Now one may refuse to consider this case, one may dismiss it out of hand as Ramsey is disposed to do simply by excluding it from the realm of "concrete policy," but in doing so one also dismisses the most important conflicts that arise among men. An analysis that declares in effect that it will not consider hegemonial struggles, that it will not deal with conflicts in which the motives of vain-glory and of survival are inextricably mixed yet all important, is largely irrelevant to the present period of state relations, not to speak of other periods. Nor can one get around this criticism by using such question-begging terms, as does Ramsey, as *political* limits," "controlling objectives," "choiceworthy political effects," etc. If these terms are intended to rule out of order conflicts in which the desire to be first or in which the desire to survive are paramount, what point can they have when these are precisely the critical conflicts with which we must deal? And even if we take these terms seriously, to argue, for example, that

34

doing evil beyond reasonable limit, even on the basis of its own presuppositions it must rely on the threat to do evil. That this threat is for the most part implicit rather than explicit, that it largely inheres in the nature of the weapons themselves and men's inability to predict the consequences of using these weapons rather than in the overt threat to use them in a certain manner, does not alter matters. The expectations men entertain of the way in which nuclear weapons would be used if deterrence failed form as much a part of the reality of deterrence, so long as these expectations persist, as do the weapons on which such expectations rest. In consequence, whatever the express articulation of deterrent strategies, so long as men continue to entertain these expectations the effectiveness of the deterrent threat will continue to rest largely on what is interpreted as a threat to do evil. And given the novelty of the weapons that form the basis of deterrent systems there is, after all, quite as much to be said for the view that the use of nuclear weapons would not and could not be confined to military objectives as there is to be said for the contrary view.

To be sure, it may be argued that even if deterrent strategies rely on the threat to do evil, that threat still does not necessarily imply an actual intent to do evil. If what is evil to do must also be evil to intend to do, however small the chance that this intent will have to be carried out, it does not follow that what is evil to intend to do must also be evil to threaten to do. Nuclear strategies may therefore rely, it is argued, on a threat to do evil that still need not betray an actual intent to do evil. And even if the moralist may question the justification of threatening to do evil, though not intending to do evil, there is still a difference between a threat of action that carries no intent to act and a threat that does do so. But all this argument succeeds in establishing is a distinction which no one would care to deny, that is, that a threat to act may be distinguished from an intent to act. It does not indicate how the threat on which deterrence is based, if only by implication, can be effectively maintained without also maintaining the intent to carry out the threat if necessary. Still less, does it indicate how, in practice, an intentless threat may be distinguished from an intentful threat without putting the threat to the one and only reliable test. In the absence of this test, however, it must be admitted that the argument cannot be conclusively disproved. All that can be said, though it seems quite enough, is that in the absence of very strong

---

hegemony or survival are not "choiceworthy political effects" is, to say the least, a rather curious reading of history. If, however, we read history more normally they are not only the effects men have most desired, but also the effects which render the element of will supremely important.

evidence to the contrary, there is no reason to assume that a threat to do evil does not also imply an intent to do evil.[24]

The conclusion to which these considerations lead is that if we are not deliberately to press *bellum justum* into the mold of reason

---

[24] These remarks ought not to be interpreted as an acceptance of the view that what is evil to do is also evil to threaten to do, and to intend to do, whatever the consequences of refusing to threaten evil and however small the chance that the threat will ever have to be acted on. It is not self-evident why what must be evil to do must also be evil to threaten to do, and to intend to do, apart from the circumstances attending and the consequences following this threat. For the Christian moralist, however, it is self-evident. One must never intend to do evil simply because one ought never to entertain an evil intent. The view that if an act would be evil to do it must also be evil to intend to do may take several forms. In its pure form, one must never intend to do evil simply because one ought never to entertain an evil intent, and this quite apart either from the prospect that the intent will have to be acted on or from the consequences the intent (not the action) may have for those who entertain it. In its less than pure form, one must never intend to do evil because of the possibility that at some time, in some circumstances, one will do evil. Finally, there is the argument that even if the intent may never have to be acted on, one ought never to intend to do evil in view of the debilitating consequences that entertaining this intent will have for its possessor. In its pure form, then, the injunction against intending evil is evidently independent of calculation and consequence, whereas in its impure forms this injunction is just as evidently dependent on calculation and consequence. Moreover, in its impure forms this injunction is open to question when applied to a given situation precisely because it is dependent on calculation and consequence. Thus the condemnation of strategies of deterrence which are based on these impure, or less than absolute, versions of the injunction against doing evil are open to challenge and to possible rejection on their own chosen grounds. It may well be, for example, that the possibility of deterrent strategies breaking down is so small as to be negligible. And if this possibility is negligible, or is believed to be negligible, the consequences of holding this intent may not prove debilitating at all for the holders. Even if this possibility is not believed to be negligible, it may not prove debilitating. Indeed, what evidence there is seems to point to the conclusion that, on the whole, deterrent strategies have not proven debilitating for those societies maintaining them. At any rate, the argument from consequences is dependent on an examination of consequences, so far as we are in a position to do so, and a weighing of these consequences against the possible consequences of abandoning a deterrent strategy. By implication, it also involves a comparison of the values gained and sacrificed by each set of consequences and the making of a choice. But this must mean that the values involved, including the value of avoiding the intent to do evil, are only relative in character. In marked contrast, the Christian moralists who insist on the pure form of the injunction against intending to do evil must unreservedly condemn deterrent strategies, if the considerations put forth in the text above are sound. Even if deterrence is acknowledged as a means to a very desired end (world peace), and even if deterrence is acknowledged to operate with something akin to certainty, particularly if the threat is made sufficiently horrendous, it must nevertheless be con-

of state there is an irreconcilable conflict between the requirement of *bellum justum* and the requirement of deterrent strategies. This conclusion is not prompted in the first place by the unpersuasive character of the attempts that have been made to reconcile possible deterrent strategies with the requirements on means laid down by *bellum justum*.[25] Even if these attempts were more persuasive than they are they would fail in what must be their fundamental purpose, which is to show that in principle as well as in practice such reconciliation is possible. It is not enough to demonstrate that a hypothetical deterrent strategy or an equally hypothetical strategy for waging thermonuclear war may just possibly be made compatible with *bellum justum*. What must instead be shown is that the limiting conditions which may just possibly establish this compatibility can also be made, as a matter of principle and of practice, politically effective yet remain self-contained. No one has shown this, however, and it is altogether unlikely that anyone will be able to show this. All that can be shown is that the principal, and apparently the indispensable, sanction for the limits required of the just war, nuclear or otherwise, remains the meaningful threat of nuclear war which clearly exceeds these limits.[26]

---

demned if it implies the intent to do evil. Given the consequences that would probably follow from the condemnation of deterrence, if such condemnation were acted upon, the understandable reluctance on the part of many moralists to avoid that result has been productive of ingenuous efforts toward condoning deterrence yet insisting upon the pure form of the principle that evil may never be intended that good may come. The "psychology of deterrence" of course encourages such efforts. Thus, in addition to the distinction drawn between threat and intent, discussed above, it has been urged that deterrence requires us to distinguish between an interim and a final or ultimate intention. According to this argument, there is no ultimate evil intention involved in deterrence, only an interim intention to do evil. Paradoxically, one's ultimate intention can be free from evil only if one's interim intention is evil. If I really intend to do evil, and the adversary knows I really intend to do evil, I will never have to do evil. My interim intent not only saves me from having to carry out this intent; the knowledge of this permits me ultimately not to intend to do evil at all.

There is no end to this sort of casuistry. However much these efforts may elicit our admiration, and even sympathy, they fail to persuade.

[25] We must emphasize the term "possible," since "actual" deterrent strategies are expressly based on the threat of attacking, if necessary, civilian populations. We have no reason to suppose that this threat does not correspond to real intent.

[26] A very different view of the possibility of reconciling the requirements of *bellum justum* with the requirements of nuclear deterrence is taken by Paul Ramsey, *The Limits of Nuclear War* and "More Unsolicited Advice to Vatican Council II." Ramsey believes such reconciliation is possible, if we distinguish with sufficient clarity between a "declared" and a "real" intention and if we assess correctly the "shared deterrence in the collateral damage inflicted by use of

There is no way, then, by which the present circle can be squared, no way by which the necessities of the nuclear power can be acknowledged yet the measures by which these necessities may be preserved always limited. In principle, there has never been a way by which the state's necessities can be acknowledged yet the measures by which these necessities may be preserved always limited. Nuclear weapons have not created this dilemma, they have simply illuminated it as never before and given it greater poignancy than men ever thought possible. Even so, whether and to what extent the require-

---

nuclear weapons over legitimate targets only." Although both points have been dealt with in the text, some additional remarks on the second point are in order. Ramsey's collateral damage is mainly the damage inflicted on noncombatants in the course of attacking military objectives. It is, in his view, not only an effective form of deterrence ("mutual and enough, without ever thinking of executing city-hostages") but a just form of deterrence ("Legitimate deterrence is the indirect effect of the unavoidable indirect effects [collateral civil damage] of properly targeted and therefore justly intended and justly conducted war in the nuclear age.") "More Unsolicited Advice . . .," pp. 46–47. We must ask, however, if purely counterforce deterrence has been "mutual and enough" why haven't nuclear powers been satisfied with it? The answer, it would appear, is that whereas the statesman knows that the limitation of violence is ultimately dependent on the threat of unlimited violence, Ramsey refuses to acknowledge this dependency. Besides, how limited is the nuclear war, hence the deterrent intent, Ramsey does consider compatible with *bellum justum*? Expert testimony indicates that between major nuclear powers a nuclear war limited to counterforces may still be expected to result in the deaths of perhaps a majority of the population of the participants. Even if we were to accept the view that this "indirect effect" of killing half a population would not be the doing of evil, there would remain the question of the proportionality of the action. Ramsey has correctly pointed out the indeterminacy of the test of proportionality. But if we are to retain this test at all, and we can scarcely discard it, the admitted indeterminacy of proportionality cannot be simply caricatured. If there is a point beyond which the sheer destruction of nuclear war becomes disproportionate to any good sought, where does Ramsey draw this line? To answer by declaring that the line cannot be drawn in advance is to permit, if only by implication, the death and injury of any portion of an adversary's noncombatant population so long as this death and injury is the presumed indirect effect of properly targeted weapons. Finally, and perhaps most importantly, the question arises whether Ramsey's use of "collateral" effects, in terms of indirect civil damage, is not a clear abuse of the principle of double-effect, in the sense that this principle is understood by Ramsey as well as by other Christian moralists. In a critique of Ramsey's position on collateral damage, Walter Stein correctly identifies this abuse: "The decisive flaw in Ramsey's position is the dependence of his supposed 'collateral deterrence' upon effects essential to the purpose of nuclear strategy, directly indispensable, radically wanted—and yet to be sanctioned as 'side-effects.'" "The Limits of Nuclear War: Is a Just Deterrence Strategy Possible?" in *Peace, the Churches and the Bomb*, p. 81.

ments of *bellum justum* are reconcilable in practice with the necessities of the state has always been conditioned by circumstances. When circumstance has permitted a reconciliation in practice, the reconciliation has nevertheless been made possible by the meaningful, if perhaps unobtrusive and unoppressive, prospect of conflict that must exceed the limits of the just war. The age-old institution of reprisal is but the most obvious illustration of this truth that the possibility of restraint in statecraft has been ultimately grounded in the possibility of a lack of restraint, or, in the terms of *bellum justum,* that the possibility of not doing evil has been ultimately grounded in the possibility of doing evil. Nevertheless, it is true that in the case of strategies of nuclear deterrence, the threat to do evil is more obtrusive and oppressive than ever before. It is also true that the dilemma which in practice could once be left in abeyance by those who insist that the state's necessities must always remain limited can no longer be left in abeyance.

Thus it is particularly in the nuclear age that it is the fate of *bellum justum* either to risk political irrelevance or to risk sacrificing its distinctive claim in order to remain politically relevant. If the injunction against doing evil that good may come is taken seriously the price is political irrelevance. If *bellum justum* is to remain politically relevant, the price is the erosion of the significance of "doing evil." For political relevance can be ultimately insured only by acceptance of the constituent principle of statecraft, which is that of reciprocity or retribution. Given the circumstances in which statecraft is conducted, the rejection of this principle is tantamount to the rejection of statecraft itself. Yet it is precisely this principle that *bellum justum* must reject if it is to set limits to the necessities of state. That the point in practice at which the latent antagonism between the injunction against doing, or threatening, evil and the principle of "like for like" must become overt cannot be determined in the abstract and with certainty does not mean that it cannot be determined at all. That it depends upon circumstances and a judgment that may always prove fallible does not warrant the conclusion that it is therefore non-existent. Whoever takes this position must refuse to acknowledge that in practice it is scarcely possible to identify the doing of evil at all.

The Just War and Vatican II

In the light of the foregoing analysis, what may we say of the statement on war in the Pastoral Constitution on "The Church in the

Modern World," adopted by the Second Vatican Council?[27] Our reply to this question can be summarily stated at the outset. The Council's position on war does not appear to deviate substantially from what has been earlier described as the prevailing twentieth century reconstruction of *bellum justum*. In consequence, the ambiguities inherent in this modern reconstruction are equally inherent in the position taken by the Council. Finally, the critical issues raised by the prospect of nuclear war and, more importantly, by existing strategies of deterrence are left by the Council largely as they were found.

This assessment of the Council's work will scarcely be challenged with respect to the position taken on the right of states to have recourse to armed force. The Council appears to adopt as its own the prevailing modern version of the *jus ad bellum* in declaring that: "As long as the danger of war remains and there is no competent and sufficiently powerful authority at the international level, governments cannot be denied the right to legitimate defense once every means of peaceful settlement has been exhausted." A literal interpretation of this right, it is true, does not exclude a measure of doubt over its meaning. A "right to legitimate defense" need not be construed as a right to have recourse to armed force only to protect the state's self—its territorial integrity and political independence—against unjust attack. A "right to legitimate defense" may be interpreted as a right to use armed force not only to defend the state's "self" but also to defend other rights of the state as well. Thus the statement may be understood to comprise a right to employ armed force not only as a measure of legitimate self-defense but, more generally, as a measure of legitimate self-help taken in response to other injuries done to a state, injuries in response to which alternative means of self-redress prove unavailing and unsatisfactory. But if this latter interpretation is not excluded, it is hardly a reasonable interpretation in view of the developments we have already noted. There is no sufficient reason to assume that the Council intended to arrest, and even to reverse, these developments by reaffirming, in effect, the *jus ad bellum* of the classic doctrine. Moreover, in a statement that shortly follows the statement quoted above, the Council speaks of being "compelled" to undertake an evaluation of war with an "entirely new attitude." In

---

[27] Cf. Second Vatican Council, *Pastoral Constitution on the Church in the Modern World, December 7, 1965* (National Catholic Welfare Conference, 1966). The Council's statement on war appears in Part II, Chapter V. In the following analysis we have chosen to concentrate on those issues developed in earlier pages. A number of significant issues raised by the Council's statement are thereby neglected.

part, at least, it seems clear that this "entirely new attitude" consists in restricting the just war to the war of legitimate self-defense.[28]

If the Council limits the just war to the war of legitimate self-defense, it does not have a great deal to say about the meaning and scope of this one remaining justification for war. The persisting uncertainty and controversy over the rights on behalf of which, and the acts in response to which, forcible measures of self-defense may be justly undertaken are scarcely considered. What the Council does address itself to are the general conditions or requirements that must be observed in exercising the right of legitimate defense. Although this right "cannot be denied" states, it may only be exercised "once every means of peaceful settlement has been exhausted." Since war, and particularly modern war, is an evil to be avoided whenever possible, this duty to exhaust every means of peaceful settlement must be taken with the utmost seriousness. Those who share public responsibility are therefore reminded that they have the duty "to conduct such grave matters soberly and to protect the welfare of the people entrusted to their care." If armed force nevertheless remains the only recourse open to a government, those who share public responsibility are further admonished that "it is one thing to undertake military action for the just defense of the people, and something else again to seek the subjugation of other nations. Nor, by the same token, does the mere fact that war has unhappily begun mean that all is fair between the warring parties."

These conditions of necessity, of right intention and of the limitation of means are also the conditions of war found in the traditional doctrine, conditions the traditional doctrine applied to just wars of "aggression" as well as to just wars of "defense."[29] The Council does not expressly refer to a further condition of the traditional doctrine and, of course, of modern versions of *bellum justum* as well, that is,

---

[28] Moreover, in a note to the Council's statement on undertaking the evaluation of war with an "entirely new attitude" the following statement from John XXIII's *Pacem in Terris* is cited: "Therefore in this age of ours which prides itself on its atomic power, it is irrational to believe that war is still an apt means of vindicating violated rights."

[29] In part, of course, a change has occurred in the meaning given to right intention. Although it is true that the *recta intentio* of the traditional doctrine proscribed what the Council statement proscribes ("to seek the subjugation of other nations"), it permitted, and even stressed, the desire to punish the wicked. This punitive element no longer characterizes modern versions of *bellum justum*. If anything, this element is expressly disavowed in the contemporary reconstruction of the doctrine.

41

the condition or requirement of proportionality. There is no apparent reason for assuming that this omission of an express reference to the principle of proportion is significant. Perhaps the Council considered this condition so self-evident as not to require express reiteration. Perhaps the Council considered that the principle of proportion was implicit almost throughout the Council's statement on the avoidance of war, that it implicitly formed a large part of the rationale on which the Council's statement rested, and for this reason needed no explicit reference. Whatever the reason, the omission is interesting, if not significant, in view of the prominence usually accorded the principle of proportion in previous utterances of the Church and, more generally, in the writings on war of Christian moralists.

We have earlier argued that if we are to find a distinctive quality in *bellum justum,* a quality that sets clear and meaningful limits to the necessities of the state, this quality must be found in the restraints placed on the conduct or means of war. Whereas reason of state must reject the claim that there are inherent limits on the means that may be threatened or employed to preserve the state, *bellum justum* must insist that there are such limits and that whatever the circumstances these limits may never be transgressed. The Council, too, places great emphasis on the intrinsic limits that men must observe in their actions, including—or especially—their actions in war, in declaring that: ". . . the Council wishes, above all things else, to recall the permanent binding force of universal natural law and its all-embracing principles. Man's conscience itself gives ever more emphatic voice to these principles. Therefore, actions which deliberately conflict with these same principles, as well as orders commanding such actions are criminal, and blind obedience cannot excuse those who yield to them."

This is, indeed, a very uncompromising statement of principle. It reasserts, and reasserts in the most emphatic manner, that there are limits to the necessities of the state, limits that may never be transgressed. How is this statement of principle applied to the conduct of states, particularly in war? Does it set clear and meaningful limits to the measures men may take, whatever the circumstances and whatever the alleged necessities of the state? Does it forbid, is it interpreted by the Council to forbid, the doing, or the threatening, of evil that good may come?

There is no simple answer to these questions. There is no simple answer largely for the reasons that there was no simple answer to the same questions when considered in an earlier context. However uncompromising the statement of principle made by the Council, in itself this statement does not afford us much guidance with respect to the conduct which is absolutely forbidden. Genocide apart,[30] there is one, and only one, action that elicits the Council's unqualified moral condemnation. It is set forth in these words:

> . . . this most Holy Synod makes its own the condemnations of total war already pronounced by recent popes, and issues the following declaration:
> Any act of war aimed indiscriminately at the destruction of entire cities or extensive areas along with their population is a crime against God and man himself. It merits unequivocal and unhesitating condemnation.

How are we to interpret this most solemn declaration by the Council? What is the behavior or action that is forbidden and why is it forbidden? The two questions are, of course, closely related. In neither case, however, is the answer altogether clear. This uncertainty is particularly apparent when we examine the rationale for the Council's declaration. To be sure, for those who interpret the Council's declaration to mean the reassertion of the moral immunity of non-combatants from direct attack, the why of this declaration is entirely clear. On this view, the Council has simply and forcibly reaffirmed the essential difference between war and murder; it has said that the deliberate killing of the innocent must always be avoided, that this killing may never be justified even as a reprisal measure taken in response to similar measures of an adversary. But if this interpretation is correct why did the Council not affirm the rights of the innocent even more simply and directly by stating in traditional terms the principle of noncombatant immunity from direct attack? That principle may surely be violated, and seriously violated, by acts which fall well short of the indiscriminate destruction of "entire cities or extensive areas." Moreover, if the Council simply intended by this most solemn declaration to reassert the principle of non-combatant immunity, one might not unreasonably have expected it to go a good deal beyond this in the acts it condemned, and to do so even in the context of a discussion of the "horror and perversity" of modern warfare. That the Council does not do so leaves open the possible interpretation that it condemns total war and any act of war aimed indiscriminately at the destruction of entire cities or extensive areas primarily for the reason that these acts violate the requirement of proportionality, that the evil attending the commission of these acts

---

[30] The Council does not actually use the term genocide. Instead, it condemns as the "most infamous" among the actions which deliberately conflict with universal natural law those actions "designed for the methodical extermination of an entire people, nation or ethnic minority."

is disproportionate to the good resulting from them. It is also possible to interpret the Council's condemnation to imply that the acts condemned are so condemned because their commission, in addition to violating the principle of proportion, is not compatible with a defensive war. On this latter view, total war and acts aimed indiscriminately at the destruction of entire cities must be condemned for the additional reason that even though subjectively undertaken only in self-defense their objective effect is to lead either to the subjugation or the annihilation of the adversary.[31]

There are, then, at least three possible interpretations of the rationale for this most solemn declaration by the second Vatican Council. Even if we accept the first interpretation as the most plausible, there remains the question of the significance of this presumed

---

[31] The Council introduces the declaration under discussion by the words "with these truths in mind." In doing so, the Council evidently refers, in large part, to these statements made in an immediately preceding paragraph: "The horror and perversity of war is immensely magnified by the increase in the number of scientific weapons. For acts of war involving these weapons can inflict massive and indiscriminate destruction, thus going far beyond the bounds of legitimate defense. Indeed, if the kind of instruments which can now be found in the armories of the great nations were to be employed to their fullest, an almost total and altogether reciprocal slaughter of each side by the other would follow, not to mention the widespread devastation that would take place in the world and the deadly after-effects that would be spawned by the use of weapons of this kind." In introducing its most solemn declaration with "these truths in mind," the Council provides further support for the possible interpretation that the acts in question are condemned not only, and not even primarily, because they violate the principle of noncombatant immunity but because they violate the requirement of proportionality and go beyond the bounds of a defensive war. — It is also worth noting that one of the "truths" endorsed by the Council is not always true except in a definitional sense. If "legitimate defense" is understood to imply defense by certain means and not by others, and if the means excluded are acts inflicting "massive and indiscriminate destruction," then it is by definition true that acts inflicting such destruction "thus" go beyond the bounds of legitimate defense. It is doubtful, however, that this is all the Council intended to say. More probably, the Council intended to imply by its "truth" that acts inflicting massive and indiscriminate destruction are neither legitimate (in the definitional sense) nor defensive (in the sense of ever proving necessary for a state's defense). This latter contention is not always true. A state may employ forbidden means— including the means in question—and nevertheless wage a war that, in terms of causes and ends, is strictly defensive. If the just war must now be a war fought only in self-defense against unjust attack, it does not necessarily follow that a strictly defensive war, in terms of causes and ends, is a just war. The Council does not quite face up to the difficulties these considerations must raise. Instead, it manages to avoid them by presenting the limiting case in which war would be neither defensive nor just.

reasserton of the principle of noncombatant immunity in terms of the acts that are absolutely forbidden. Literally, what is condemned by the Council is not any act that involves the direct and intentional attack on the innocent. Nor is it even true to say that what is expressly condemned is an indiscriminate act of war. Apart from "total war," what the Council expressly condemns is not indiscriminate action as such but "any act of war aimed indiscriminately at the destruction of entire cities or extensive areas along with their population."[32] We cannot but call attention to these words: "entire cities" and "extensive areas." Is this the simple and forcible reassertion of the moral immunity of noncombatants from direct and intentional attack or is it the near emasculation of this immunity?

It may of course be argued that these considerations, and the criticism they evidently imply, miss the point. In expressly forbidding what it does expressly forbid, and forbids absolutely, the Council's declaration should not be interpreted as permitting any and all actions that fall short of these forbidden actions. What the Council does not expressly condemn it does not, for that reason, thereby permit. What men do in war, no less than what they do in peace, is subject to, in the Council's words, "the permanent binding force of universal natural law and its all-embracing principles." If one of the most important of these universal and all-embracing principles is the prohibition of murder—the deliberate killing of the innocent—the Council can hardly be criticized for not having expressly condemned behavior it evidently intended and must have intended to condemn. But even if we accept this argument, we are still left with all of the issues raised in earlier pages. Apart from condemning what it does expressly condemn, the Council does not address itself to these issues. Instead, it has for the most part simply left these issues where it found them.

These considerations should not be pushed too far. If the Council has not simply and forcibly reasserted the principle of noncombatant

---

[32] We do not seriously consider a further ambiguity in the declaration, an ambiguity that is almost certainly the result of technically poor drafting or of an inadequate translation of the original text. The Council forbids "any act of war aimed indiscriminately at the destruction of entire cities . . ." Logically, this leaves open the possibility that any act of war "aimed discriminately at the destruction of entire cities" may not be forbidden, unless, of course, the destruction of cities is, by definition, an indiscriminate act. If it is so defined, and we may assume that this definition is implied, then the statement as it stands in its English version is simply redundant rather than ambiguous. Instead, it should have read: "any act of war aimed at the destruction of entire cities . . . is indiscriminate and is a crime against God and man himself."

immunity from direct and intentional attack, it also has not abandoned that principle. If the Council has not reconciled the necessities of any war, and particularly of nuclear war, with the injunction against doing evil, it has insisted that there are at least some necessities that can never be justified, some means that may never be permitted, and accordingly, some evil that may never be done. It may be true that the acts the Council condemns are of such a character that their condemnation can hardly afford much comfort. The fact remains that these acts may express, and in certain circumstances undoubtedly do express, the necessities of the nuclear Power. Moreover, the Council, while clearly not condemning the use of nuclear weapons and other "scientific weapons," goes very far in expressing its skepticism that these weapons can in actual practice be justly employed.

The Council does not content itself merely with pointing out that these weapons "*can* inflict massive and indiscriminate destruction" but goes on to state: "The unique hazard of modern warfare consists in this: it provides those who possess modern scientific weapons with a kind of occasion for perpetrating just such abominations [i.e., the indiscriminate destruction of entire cities or extensive areas]; moreover, through a certain inexorable chain of events, it can catapult men into the most atrocious decisions." What can this passage mean save that scientific weapons severely limit the freedom men formerly enjoyed in war, a freedom to control and to limit their actions, and that they do so not because, or not primarily because, of their nature but because of man's nature. The "kind of occasion" these weapons provide their possessors, if once employed, does not constitute a necessity in the literal sense. It is a kind of occasion, however, which in practice might well prove indistinguishable from just such a necessity.

The weapons that provide a "kind of occasion" for perpetrating abominations in war also provide a way by which, in the Council's words, "peace of a sort" can be maintained. What has the Council to say about this peace of deterrence? The importance of the Council's position on deterrence need not be labored. Nuclear war is a possibility and increasingly in the view of most observers only a remote possibility. Deterrence is the reality in which we live at present and the reality in which we are very likely to continue living for a considerable time. The necessities of the nuclear state do not find their principal manifestation today in that dreaded, but hopefully remote, possibility of nuclear war. They do find their principal manifestation in deterrence. It is clear, then, that the significance of this most recent expression of the Christian response to the ancient plea of reason of state must largely be found in the Council's position on deterrence, the substance of which is found in the following paragraphs:

> Scientific weapons, to be sure, are not amassed solely for use in war. Since the defensive strength of any nation is considered to be dependent upon its capacity for immediate retaliation, this accumulation of arms, which increases every year, likewise serves, in a way heretofore unknown, as a deterrent to possible enemy attack. Many regard this as the most effective way by which peace of a sort can be maintained between nations at the present time.
>
> Whatever be the facts about this method of deterrence, men should be convinced that the arms race in which an already considerable number of countries are engaged is not a safe way to preserve a steady peace, nor is the so-called balance resulting from this race a sure and authentic peace. Rather than being eliminated thereby, the causes of war are in danger of being gradually aggravated. While extravagant sums are being spent for the furnishing of ever new weapons, an adequate remedy cannot be provided for the multiple miseries afflicting the whole modern world. Disagreements between nations are not really and radically healed; on the contrary, they spread the infection to other parts of the earth. New approaches based on reformed attitudes must be taken to remove this trap and to emancipate the world from its crushing anxiety through the restoration of genuine peace.

The reader can only sympathize with the hardships under which the drafters of this statement labored to reconcile positions that are, in the last analysis, irreconcilable. At the same time, he must remain frustrated by the studied ambiguity that appears to characterize the result of these labors. The Council declares that "many regard" the accumulation of arms for immediate retaliation against aggressive attack "the most effective way by which peace of a sort" can presently be maintained. Does the Council share this regard? It will not say so. Yet it does say that this accumulation of arms serves as a deterrent "in a way heretofore unknown." Does this imply indirect acceptance of what "many regard"? One cannot be sure. The Council disavows knowledge of the facts of deterrence ("whatever be the facts about this method of deterrence"). Yet it declares that "men should be convinced that the arms race . . . is not a safe way to preserve a steady peace . . ."[33] Why should men be so convinced, whatever be

---

[33] The sense of this statement is, in any event, far from clear. Is the Council merely saying that there are, in principle, safer ways to preserve a steadier peace? If so, the point seems curiously out of place, since it borders on levity. On the other hand, if the Council is saying that in the world in which we presently live, a world the Council describes elsewhere so profoundly, there are available safer

the facts? Again, the Council implies that "this method of deterrence" prevents war while aggravating the causes of war, that deterrence both lessens and increases the dangers of war. This analysis may very well be true, though one may still seriously question whether sums spent on new weapons prevent an "adequate remedy" for the "multiple miseries afflicting the modern world" just as one may question whether these multiple miseries constitute a significant cause of the war men hope to avoid. But how can the Council know all this without also knowing the facts about "this method of deterrence"?

It is not with the ambiguities marking the Council's analysis of deterrence that we are primarily concerned, however, but with its judgment of the morality of deterrence. Whatever be the facts about this method of deterrence, what is the Council's position on the legitimacy of this method? In refusing to condemn the possession of nuclear weapons, does the Council thereby approve, however reluctantly, the possession of these weapons for deterrent purposes? It would seem so. Nor is this all. In failing to condemn strategies of deterrence that rest, and that are known to rest in the ultimate resort, upon the threat of destroying "entire cities," does the Council thereby approve, however reluctantly, these strategies? Again, it would seem so. If this is the most reasonable interpretation of the Council's position on the morality of deterrence, the substance of this position is that the means that may never be employed and the evil that may never be done may nevertheless be threatened.[34] Thus does the Coun-

---

ways to preserve a steadier peace than the peace of deterrence, this is an altogether different point and a point that many, including the present writer, would seriously controvert. Again, it is quite another matter to insist that what we presently have is not a "sure and authentic peace." That the "so-called balance" resulting from the arms race and deterrence is not a "sure and authentic peace" follows from the Council's definition of a sure and authentic peace. It is painfully clear that the peace of deterrence is not a peace that is the fruit of mutual trust and of justice, let alone of love. In this sense, of course, no peace men have known has been a sure and authentic peace. Moreover, in the relations of states such peace as men have known has nearly always been based on this "so-called balance" that the Council contrasts with a sure and authentic peace. These considerations apart, it probably remains true that the peace of deterrence represents the polar extreme when compared with the peace that is based on mutual trust and a shared sense of justice, for the peace of deterrence forms the classic —one is almost tempted to say the perfect—example of the peace that is based on the principle of retribution.

[34] This interpretation of the Council's position will be contested by many. Clearly, the Council neither expressly condemns nor expressly approves the possession of nuclear weapons. It is possible, then, to interpret the Council either as implicitly condemning or implicitly approving the possession of nuclear weapons.

cil retain political relevance for *bellum justum* in an age dominated by the peace of deterrence. Thus does the Council attempt to reconcile the irreconcilable, the requirements of *bellum justum* and the necessities of a nuclear Power. And thus does the Council demonstrate once

---

(We exclude the possibility that the Council neither implicitly condemns nor implicitly approves the possession of nuclear weapons. Quite apart from the logical difficulties this alleged possibility must raise, it suggests that the Council refused to take any moral position on what is perhaps the most important issue of the day and the most important issue that confronted the Council. We do not enter the charge, indeed we reject it, that the Council thus shirked its duty by refusing to provide men with moral guidance on this critical matter.) There is very little support for the position that the Council implicitly condemned the possession of these weapons. True, the Commission responsible for the drafting struck out the statement on the next to final draft that "the deterrent possession of such arms cannot be said to be illegitimate." That statement appeared to some to come very close to expressly sanctioning the possession of these weapons and was therefore resisted. It requires a curious interpretation of the omission of that statement, however, to conclude that the Council thereby implicitly condemned the possession of nuclear weapons. Indeed, the omission of that statement from the final text does not significantly alter the meaning of the text.

If the Council implicitly approved of the possession of nuclear weapons it must be further assumed that it implicitly approved, in principle, of deterrent strategies which have their basis in these weapons. The question that arises, then, and it is the central question, is whether or not the Council implicitly approved of deterrent strategies which threaten, in the last resort as a measure of reprisal, the destruction of "entire cities." Those who argue that the Council cannot be interpreted as approving such strategies point to the Council's solemn and unqualified condemnation of "total war" and of "any act of war aimed indiscriminately at the destruction of entire cities or extensive areas . . ." If the Council condemns these acts, it is contended, then it must also be understood to condemn the threat to carry out these acts and, of course, the intent to do so. We do not deny that this argument is a possible interpretation of the Council's position. We do assert that it is not the more plausible interpretation of that position. If the Council wished to condemn deterrent threats of an indiscriminate nature, why did it not do so? Nothing would have been easier than to have made a statement in the context of deterrence parallel to the statement made in the context of war. But the Council did not do so, and it did not do so knowing that strategies of deterrence rest, in the final resort, on the threat of counter-city warfare. How are we to interpret a statement that condemns, and condemns absolutely, acts which form only a hopefully remote possibility yet is silent on threats which form the reality in which we daily live?

The answer to this question, it would seem, is that the Council Fathers were faced with a true moral dilemma. The issue of deterrence raised conflicting moral demands. As between these conflicting moral demands the Council remained uncertain, hence the Delphic character of its statement on the morality of deterrence. At least, this would appear to be a reasonable interpretation of the Council's statement on deterrence. Nevertheless, it will be resisted by those moralists, and particularly by Catholic moralists, who refuse to accept the possi-

49

again that there is no way by which the circle can be squared, that there is no way by which the injunction against doing, or threatening, evil that good may come can be reconciled with the constituent principle of statecraft.

---

bility of true moral dilemmas arising. From this viewpoint, moral choice may be extremely difficult but it never gives rise to a true dilemma, the essence of which is the inability to justify a choice between moral claims that, although regarded as equally compelling, have become irreconcilable. But this viewpoint assumes that men have, or may always have, a clear hierarchy of values and that the significance of this hierarchy of values is always apparent in practice. There is no persuasive reason, however, for believing that this must always be so. Nor, indeed, does experience indicate that it is always so. Moral dilemmas may, and do, arise because men are often unable to order their moral life as neatly as this view assumes. Not only do they often give equal significance to certain ends which circumstances have made irreconcilable, they are often confronted with situations in which it is next to impossible to determine the effects of a choice, any choice, on the values they do hold.

THE *PASTORAL* CONSTITUTION

by George G. Higgins

I would like my comments to be regarded as informal reflections on the discussion which was initiated by Robert Tucker's paper. Because it was a lively and informed inter-faith discussion of the Vatican Council's treatment of the subject of war and peace in its *Pastoral Constitution on the Church in the Modern World* it had an immediately evident value. It was my impression, however, that while the group as a whole was more or less favorably impressed by the over-all tone of the document, there was a certain feeling of disappointment or regret on the part of some of the participants that the Council had stopped short of condemning (or approving) the possession of nuclear arms by the great powers and had failed to lay down final moral directives with regard to a number of other specific problems in the field of international relations.

I suspect that this feeling of disappointment or regret is fairly widespread among Catholics and non-Catholics alike. It stems, I think, from a misunderstanding of the purpose of the *Constitution on the Church in the Modern World* and the methodology employed by the Commission which was responsible for drafting it. This particular conciliar document is, by definition, a "pastoral" constitution. Its purpose is not to say the last word on current problems from the point of view of Catholic theology, but rather to call attention to certain practical steps that men of good will can take (in the case of the specific subject under discussion) to limit international conflicts and to build a stable and lasting peace.

Bishop Mark McGrath of Panama, who played a prominent role on the Commission which drafted the Constitution, explained all this to the Council Fathers last fall when he presented his "relatio" or introductory statement on the first part of the Constitution. Because of the very nature of the document, he pointed out, it was necessary that the real condition of today's world be described, at least in a general way, before any judgments were made about it. This inductive or descriptive methodology, he said, was set forth in the introductory chapter of the Constitution and was followed throughout the entire document. Finally, the Bishop noted, "the very newness of many of the questions proposed and their diversity . . . impose limits on our document. General principles, either doctrinal or moral, are proposed, which principles frequently do not touch upon completely concrete solutions either because the problems involved require more mature examination, or because they must be considered by the faithful in a particular way in each region, under the guidance of their pastors."

The same point is made in the text of the Constitution itself. It is specifically stated that the program outlined in the Constitution is a very general one and deliberately so, given the immense variety of situations and forms of human culture in the world. "Indeed," we are told, "while it presents teaching already accepted in the Church, the program will have to be followed up and amplified since it sometimes deals with matters in a constant state of development. Still, we have relied on the word of God and the spirit of the Gospel. Hence we entertain the hope that many of our proposals will prove to be of substantial benefit to everyone, especially after they have been adapted to individual nations and mentalities by the faithful under the guidance of their pastors."

The Constitution's explicit reference to the fact that mankind must search for answers to the complex questions of the modern world and that the Church wishes only to be of service to mankind in carrying out this search was echoed in Bishop McGrath's introductory statement on the methodology of the document. Thus, the Bishop stated, the introductory chapter of the Constitution "ought to serve the purpose of the entire schema: namely, to speak to the entire world, with a serious study of the problems which now concern its peoples, so that we may enter into a sincere dialogue with them, bringing forth the light of Christ, for the solace, strength, peace, and more abundant life of all men in God."

The tone of the entire Constitution, then, derives from this purpose, namely, to enter into a dialogue with the modern world, which is quite a different thing from telling the modern world how to "solve" all of the specific problems with which it is confronted. Faithful to the spirit of Pope John XXIII, the document refrains from sterile criticism of individuals and institutions and concentrates single-mindedly on its pastoral task of encouraging and motivating men of good will to move not from A to Z but from A to B to C. In taking this approach, the drafters of the document acted very wisely—or so it seems to me.

JUST WAR AND REASONS OF STATE

by Ralph Potter

There is no "non-moral approach" to the question of nuclear deterrence or to other issues of arms policy. Both the tradition of *bellum justum* and the doctrine of "reason of state" presuppose certain moral commitments. We cannot consider one to be "a moral view" while the other is simply "descriptive." Robert Tucker cannot properly distinguish the two theories he has isolated on the grounds that *bellum justum* imports and superimposes prior moral preferences upon the policy-making process while "reason of state" simply flows directly from sophisticated empirical analysis of the raw political facts.

"Reason of state" stands over against *bellum justum* as an alternative mode of defining the nature of true statecraft. It is not a purely descriptive or morally neutral concept. It is a normative doctrine reflecting a particular set of moral preferences. It differs from *bellum justum* not because it is unencumbered with moral elements, but because it offers a different account of the moral purposes and limits of statecraft.

Tucker explicates the normative moral elements of "reason of state" only *sotto voce*, as in footnote seventeen (p. 21): "The statesman has as his highest moral imperative the preservation of the state entrusted to his care." Such normative judgments concerning what the statesman *ought* to do, do not spring directly from observation of the customary behavior of political leaders. This type of statement should be distinguished from *historical generalizations* concerning the way political communities actually have behaved and from *psychological surmises* about the forces which impel statesmen, whether they be seen as "lust for power," "honor," "grandeur," or "responsibility." Normative ethical statements must also be distinguished from *descriptive ethical analyses* purporting to show how men have reasoned, how they have assessed the rightness and wrongness of proposed actions.

The failure to distinguish carefully among these various types of statements has enabled Tucker to invest his criticism of *bellum justum* with the prestige of hard-headed descriptive realism. His rendition of the "necessities of state" is first presented as a purely descriptive account of the way things have always been. The view "emanates from the state itself" (p. 7). It is made to appear as if on the basis of straightforward observation one could determine that "the constituent principle of statecraft" is "that of reciprocity of retribution" (p. 39). What begins as an historically descriptive generalization, open to historical dispute, evolves into a doctrine concerning how things are, how they must continue to be, and finally, how they *ought* to be.

Having taken for granted his own definition of the essential nature of statecraft, Tucker argues that rigorous application of the norms of *bellum justum* would be incompatible with the necessities of statecraft *thus defined*. Indeed, adherence to those norms would require the abandonment of this form of statecraft.

At this point the concealed moral premise becomes operative: "The statesman *ought not* to abandon this form of statecraft." Why not? Is it because, by Tucker's account, there is no other plausible form of statecraft? Even if this were so, what loss would be suffered in the abandonment of the statecraft of the "reason of state"?

For Tucker the loss would be severe. Denied the flexibility of maneuver afforded by the statecraft legitimated by the philosophy of "reason of state," the existence of the state would be in jeopardy. His doctrine "presupposes as an *ultimate end* the preservation and continuity of the state" (p. 21; my italics). Hence, to contradict the philosophy and abandon the statecraft of "reason of state" is to forfeit the ultimate end—the preservation of the state.

Is this account of the ultimate end of statecraft descriptively accurate and morally sensible? Does Tucker give an adequate account of the way men reason concerning the preservation of the state? Contrary to his view, it is precisely in the limiting case, when the existence of the state is most in jeopardy, that statesmen most clearly exhibit a basically *instrumental* view of the state. Have they not been known to allow the dismantling of the political apparatus of the state in order to preserve certain *values* which might survive in the continuing society, even if it were stripped of territorial integrity and political independence? Statesmen seem to reason that the state exists in order to accomplish certain values; if the struggle for the existing state comes to mean the forfeiture of these values, they must consider surrendering. The state is sometimes a reasonable agency, but it is always a proximate end.

The claim of the state to overriding license rests upon the assumption that it is indispensable if certain more ultimate values are to be realized. In a rapidly changing situation, in which previous experience may provide few guidelines, it is more than ever necessary to draw out and indentify the values which the state seeks and serves. Only when this has been done will we be able to ask whether the state, in the form it has assumed in relatively recent history, is, in this new context, the most effective way to preserve and to promote more fundamental human values.

The doctrine of the state implicit in Tucker's critique must itself be criticized for the sake of the flexibility he seeks to preserve in statecraft. The task of statesmen is, in words quoted from the Council Fathers, "to protect the welfare of the people entrusted to their care." The statesman's task requires a flexibility of means. It is inappropriate to fetter him with a doctrine which insists that the state, rather than the welfare of the people, is the ultimate end of statecraft.

In criticizing, as excessively absolutistic, the injunction "never directly attack noncombatants," to which he has reduced the tradition of *bellum justum,* Tucker substitutes an alternative, equally absolutistic norm: "never fail to preserve the state." This injunction comes to be sanctified as the "highest moral imperative" of the statesman. Why should not the statesman be set free to consider whether the received form of the nation-state is now dysfunctional? Is it, at this juncture, the best means to ". . . provide for the common defense, promote the general welfare, and secure the blessings of liberty. . . ."? The priorities of action might change if he concludes with Pope John that there is "a structural defect which hinders" him, "that at this historical moment the present system of organization and the way its principle of authority operates on a world basis no longer correspond to the objective requirements of the universal common good" (*Pacem in Terris,* ¶ 135). Conversely, the statesman may decide that the nation-state existing in the "state of nature" remains the most feasible form of social organization. He should at least be provided with a doctrinal framework which does not foreclose the possibility of critical reflection upon the instrumental utility of the state.

The contrast between *bellum justum* and "reason of state" is thus not a contrast between a moral and a non-moral view, or between an absolutistic and a pragmatic position. It is not a contrast between doctrinaire abandonment of statecraft and courageous acceptance of statecraft. Rather, it is a contrast of two conflicting accounts, both simultaneously descriptive and normative, of the nature and ends of statecraft itself.

Tucker has, without elaborating the basis of his preference, decided in favor of one alternative view of statecraft. It is replete with moral, and even with absolute moral elements. Taking it to be only a descriptive account, and to be the only adequate descriptive account, he has employed it as the means for discrediting the rival doctrine which finds expression in *bellum justum.*

Tucker makes strenuous demands for guidance from *bellum justum.* He complains that its principles are frequently ignored or abused in practice and implies that its restrictions have seldom constituted a serious restraint upon the action of the state. He may ignore the collateral educative influence exerted even by a doctrine abused in practice. Is it fair to ask what guidance, in practice or even in theory, can be derived from the alernative view of "reason of state"? Are the decisions of the statesman less perplexing or more reliable if he "presupposes as an ultimate end the preservation and continuity of the state"?

What does the preservation of the state mean? Is it the maintenance of the territorial limits of the state? Does it rest in the continuation of the political apparatus or a particular form of government? Territorial boundaries and political forms have been changed without the demise of the state. Does the preservation of the state have to do then with the safeguarding of the ethnic or linguistic identity or cultural tradition of the populace? Such elements also seem to be less than essential. What then is the statesman called upon to preserve? What is the "self" to be maintained by those who insist upon an absolute right of the state to self-preservation?

Tucker's analysis obscures the moral nature of the state itself. The state is the agent of a "moral community." It relies upon the maintenance of a characteristic self-image and a common pledge of loyalty. A certain style of action could enter into the very identity of a state. The viability of a state could be shattered precisely by taking certain acts considered to be necessary for the preservation of its territorial integrity and political autonomy, but held to be morally obnoxious by many of its citizens. This is an observation of some significance to those forced to deal nowadays with college students who express their disillusion about American actions in Southeast Asia through a pattern of disaffiliation.

The "self" to be maintained through the absolute right of the self-preservation of the state may be a territorial and political self, but it is more certainly a moral self, a self which may preserve in its common consciousness an abhorrence of genocide or of a direct or disproportionate attack upon noncombatants. If this abhorrence is expressed forcefully in public debate, if it is expressed so forcefully that it comes to be internalized in the minds of policy-makers and institutionalized in the structure of military forces, it may function as a significant restraint upon the imperious license of the state.

56

It may be that a thoroughgoing analysis of the "preservation of the state," which would take seriously the moral dimensions of the state, would discover a system of restraints, surprisingly akin to the traditional criteria of *bellum justum,* to be "built into" the structure of meaningful political action. If the conviction of the moral structure of the universe, which underlies the tradition of natural law and finds expression in *bellum justum,* has any truth, this ultimate convergence should not be so surprising.

Tucker's discussion, however, gives no hint of an ultimate convergence. His analysis, as it is presented in this particular essay, is truncated. It stops short of defining the state and the survival of the state and specifying the values the state is meant to serve. The neglect of broader issues is significant. Would the philosophy of "reason of state" suffice to give a satisfactory account of the entire range of the problems of statecraft? The philosophical framework used for the analysis of the question of nuclear deterrence ought to be adequate also for reflection upon such issues as the right of revolution, the problem of conscientious objection, the assessment of war crimes and genocide. Can Tucker deal with these issues without drawing nigh once again to the pattern of thought he has so sharply criticized?

It is only by neglecting such questions that Tucker can make it appear as if the Vatican Fathers and other Christian moralists have some special difficulty of "squaring the circle." The problem is also his. He gives an alternative account of what the statesman should and should not do. He operates, willy-nilly, as a political philosopher and as a moralist.

As a moralist, he is burdened with extravagant hopes concerning the efficacy of moral thought in what Ernst Troeltsch referred to as "the great task of controlling and damming the historical movement, which, in itself, is simply boundless."[1] When he quotes an utterance of the Council and asks "Does it set clear and meaningful limits to the measures men take, whatever the circumstances and whatever the alleged necessities of the state?" (p. 42) or when he comments upon the principle of noncombatant immunity and observes that "what these limits must be in practice has never been clear" (p. 26), he suggests a requirement of *a priori* specificity and precision to which no conceivable moral theory could aspire. In Tucker's concept of the function of ethical terms there is something of the fundamentalist's striving for detailed and infallible knowledge and assurance. He

---

[1] *Christian Thought: Its History and Application,* New York: Meridian Books, 1957, p. 70.

demands too much—more than any moral theory could be expected to give, more than *bellum justum* claims to give, certainly more than the rival "reason of state" can give.

Tucker has other peculiarities as a moralist. He uses the term "evil" in several different senses, without due regard for the variety of metaethical theories concerning the use, proper use, and modes of justification of ethical terms. When he asserts that "it is not possible to wage war without doing evil" (p. 31) does he mean more than that it is not possible to wage war without performing acts which are "evil" in the sense that they produce consequences which are "undesirable" or even "calamitous" to their victims? According to a teleological theory, which would evaluate acts by their consequences, such deeds might be "tragic but necessary" without being "evil" in the sense of "morally reprehensible" or "wicked." It is a disservice to all participants in political debate to collapse the distinction between that which is "ideally undesirable" and that which is "morally reprehensible." It is not simply Paul Ramsey's "ingenuity of conception" on behalf of *bellum justum* which gives war "the character of an event in which ever greater evil effects may result yet apparently through no evil acts" (p. 32). All manner of teleologists and proponents of "reason of state" have vindicated the destruction of Hiroshima on the internally coherent ground that it was the best alternative open to a decision maker conscientiously seeking to limit the undesirable ("evil"$_1$) consequences of his action and was thus not a morally reprehensible ("evil"$_2$) act. On the seemingly sound assumption that he is not an absolute pacifist and given the drift of his argument, which has an affinity for the teleological view of ethics, it is difficult to understand how Tucker has arrived so directly at the conclusion that "evil must be done in war" if by "evil" he here means "morally reprehensible" or "wicked" ("evil"$_2$). If he is using the term in the sense of "that which is ideally undesirable" ("evil"$_1$) the point seems obvious in the extreme.

The task of defining what true statecraft requires and permits is by no means a burden borne only by Christians. The tradition of *bellum justum* itself has classical roots antedating the Christian era. Indeed, I believe Paul Ramsey has exaggerated the extent to which the doctrine is the precipitate of the distinctive Christian ethic of love. The extreme universalistic quality of that ethic, expressed most sharply in the injunction to love one's enemies, does give a special dimension to the problem of defining the right functions of the state.

Christians are committed to the realization of an ever more comprehensive community. No bounded state can demand their exclusive loyalty or stand for them as an ultimate end. But to what extent can the state, in turn, be expected to seek and to serve their more universalistic loyalties? What ought the church to demand of the state? What norms apply to the civil community? By what authority can Christians speak to rulers? What guidance can they claim to give?

In developing his famous typology of religious associations, Ernst Troeltsch has illustrated the variety of answers which Christian groups have given to such questions. The sect-type of association has forsworn the claim that it has been entrusted with a direct or indispensable word of counsel for the civil magistrate. Sectarians have tended to withdraw from participation in the broader society to realize within their own fellowship the pattern of holiness intended for all Christians, but for Christians only.

The church-type group, best typified by the Roman Catholic Church, has persisted in the conviction that it is the custodian of moral truths, established by God in the creation of the world, to which all men are called to conform. Out of its special insight into the nature of man, his fall, the effects of sin and grace upon him, and his vestigial capacity for justice and his temptation to injustice, the church-type is equipped to address political leaders with counsel relevant to the conduct of public affairs. It does not restrict its supervision and intervention to matters pertaining to a narrow realm of "private" morality. It seeks to permeate and shape the life of nations to bring them into closer accord with the law of nature. In so doing, the church accepts responsibility for defining the limits of the justifiable use of force and implanting such limits in the hearts and minds not only of believers, but also of all citizens, to whom appeal can be made on the basis of the natural law.

The teaching of the church need not be accepted by all to be of value to all. It preserves and proclaims a norm of public morality which provides leverage for movements which seek social justice. In differing situations, such movements may be either conservative or revolutionary. The church's tradition of natural law, and its particular expression in *bellum justum*, provides a landmark, a point of reference for all, even for those who take their bearings mainly from other quarters.

If the moral tradition of the church is now so flagrantly inadequate as Tucker contends, if the doctrine of *bellum justum* is now militarily, psychologically, and morally "irrelevant," we are all losers. For we all have been, to some extent, parasites upon the moral labor and rigor of the Roman Catholic Church. If that church is to become

59

a sect, unable or unwilling to make its counsel heard in the realm of public affairs, the doctrine of "reason of state" may come to reign without a rival. An important point of leverage against the tyrannical state or super-state will be lost.

Tucker's strand of ethical perfectionism has striking sectarian overtones. He implies that the church should be more rigorous, more clear and consistent in its condemnation of the arms policies of the major powers. Why? To satisfy a longing for verbal tidiness and to comfort those who have a low tolerance for ambiguity? The *Pastoral Constitution on the Church in the Modern World* is the work of a body which typifies, *par excellence,* Troeltsch's church-type. It has its own "reason of state" flowing out of a conception of its divine calling to be the educator of all nations. That mission may best be served by refusing Tucker's subtle invitation to take up the vocation of a sect. The sect has its own calling to radical service and sacrifice. But its mission cannot totally replace that of the church-type, which seeks involvement and accepts compromise for the sake of its leavening influence in society.

The sections of the *Pastoral Constitution* which pertain directly to arms policy matters could indeed be improved. The strictures of Tucker deserve keen attention. But the church should not retreat into the realm of private morality or into the sanctuary of sectarianism if its teaching concerning *bellum justum* cannot fully meet the extravagant demands set by Tucker. If the doctrine seems to be exhausted when extended to reach the limiting case of nuclear deterrence, we might properly conclude that we have here approached the present limits of the clarifying power of moral discourse. There is no need to forego the gains made en route to this extreme boundary of moral comprehension. There is surely no warrant for forsaking *bellum justum* for a philosophy which breaks down nearer to the starting line of the moral trek.

Let the moral theologians profit from Tucker's careful scrutiny, but let them not be disbarred or dissuaded from the common effort to define the proper limits and restraints of statecraft. Tucker concedes that this task must be performed. His critique is an appeal that it be done better. If the theologians were to fall silent, Tucker himself would have to assume the burden of constructive work designed to build limits against the excesses of men and nations. Where would he turn? It is difficult not to assume that when he had wrestled with the entire range of problems of public life he would evolve a doctrinal framework not dissimilar to the one he has so acutely criticized with respect to the dilemma of deterrence.

The real legacy of Christian culture is a sense of moral discrepancy, a feeling that things are not as they ought to be or necessarily must be. Tucker himself evinces this sense of discrepancy. But he has been unable to give us an account of its origins or the means of its overcoming. We may turn the tables on the critics and observe that this is the danger of allowing non-theologians to dabble in public affairs!

WHICH VERSION OF JUST WAR?

by Richard H. Cox

The purpose of my comments is to raise a question about one, and only one, aspect of Professor Tucker's paper. That aspect is the way in which he develops the concept of *bellum justum.*

I

Tucker's method of treating the doctrine of *bellum justum* strikes me as depending, to a considerable extent, on the tacit use of "ideal-type" analysis. I can perhaps best explain what I mean by this by comparing what one *could* do, to what Tucker appears to me actually to do. One could, for example, begin by selecting several quite specific but different versions of the doctrine of *bellum justum.* Let us say, for the sake of argument, that one were to choose a version developed by a Protestant thinker, one by a Catholic thinker, and one by a non-religious moral philosopher. One could then summarize and compare, in some detail, the main points of such doctrines. One could go on, perhaps, to analyze and then to criticize the various doctrines with respect to the nature and validity of the premises employed, or with respect to the question of internal consistency.

Tucker chooses, instead, a more difficult and, at least to me, a more problematic way: He sets up, from the outset, a contrast between *the* doctrine of *bellum justum* and *the* doctrine of reason of state; and he claims, ultimately, to discover an irreducible opposition or tension between the two doctrines as such. Hence, his striking and repeated use of the image of the difficulty of "squaring the circle," that is the ultimate impossibility of reconciling the two without destroying the central meaning of *bellum justum,* and therefore negating its restraint, in principle, on the actions of states.

The ultimate opposition of the two doctrines depends, it seems, on the proposition that an appeal to "necessity" is essential to the doctrine of reason of state, whereas an appeal to some "absolute" moral limit—such as the principle that there may never be an attack of a deliberate and direct kind on noncombatants—is essential to the doctrine of *bellum justum*. Now since "necessity," as reason of state, presumably is itself an "absolute," it questions the validity, or even denies the existence of, any absolute moral limits on state action. But to deny that *bellum justum* contains an absolute moral limit is, in effect, according to Tucker, to "press *bellum justum* into the mold of reason of state" (p. 36).

The problem, then, of reconciling the two doctrines is an "intractable" one at the level of doctrine as such. And on the other hand, such reconciliation as may conceivably take place in the realm of "practice" has, according to Tucker, "always been conditioned by circumstance" (p. 39). This seems to mean, if I understand him correctly, that every even approximately tenable reconciliation is, in the final analysis, a largely *ad hoc* adjustment to circumstances, not a resolution of the conflict of principle between the essential element of reason of state and the essential element of *bellum justum*. Thus, in the conclusion to his general treatment, Tucker says: "In principle, there has *never* been a way by which the state's necessities can be acknowledged yet the measures by which these necessities may be preserved *always limited*" (p. 38; my italics).

II

The great intellectual attractiveness of Tucker's method of treating the problem of *bellum justum* is that it so clearly and sharply focusses on what is held to be the irreducible element of the doctrine by opposing it to what is held to be the irreducible element of its chief doctrinal opponent. But in spite of, or rather probably because of, this sharp focussing on allegedly irreducible, "ideal-type" elements, I find the method of treatment to be problematic. I find it problematic first, because of its high degree of abstraction from specific political doctrines, whether theologically or philosophically based; and second, because of a parallel but not identical way of abstracting from the way in which political leaders actually view the problem of reconciling different principles that may and often do compete in shaping the conduct of foreign policy. I must of necessity limit my explanation of these two points to very summary statements; but I hope that the general tendency of my remarks helps to throw into relief a certain quality of the argument in the paper which I have found troubling.

The first point may be illustrated by noting that in traditional Western political thought—that is, the theories or doctrines of men such as Aristotle, St. Augustine, St. Thomas Aquinas, Hugo Grotius, and John Locke—there does not appear to be a single, systematic and exclusive theory of either reason of state or *bellum justum* as such. By this I mean that what Professor Tucker refers to as *the* doctrine of reason of state, or *the* doctrine of *bellum justum* is, in fact, but an aspect of a more comprehensive treatment of political phenomena. Thus in Grotius, for example, it is true that there is an extended effort to distinguish just from unjust war; and this is done in reference to, among other competing principles, the principle of classical conventionalism according to which there is no such thing as justice *by nature*. But what is important, for our present purposes, is that the concept of a just war is itself integrated into a much more complex whole: Grotius does not, so far as I can see, attempt anything like a reduction of the concept to a kind of ideal-type. Or let us take another example, on the other side. If one says, as some do— though Tucker does not explicitly say so, I grant—that Machiavelli's political thought represents the prototype of the doctrine of "reason of state," I would demur on the following grounds. First, Machiavelli does not himself so characterize his thought. Second, to reduce his thought to a single, abstractly categorized form runs the risk of abstracting from the complexity and subtlety of that thought in a progressively arbitrary way. Furthermore, such abstracting then tends to become the rule, rather than the exception: witness the way in which it is fairly common today to categorize all political theory as essentially either "idealist" or "realist," or a hybrid of the two prototypes. These kinds of concepts are roughly analogous, I think, to the contrast of a doctrine of *bellum justum* with a doctrine of reason of state. And in both cases, it seems to me that a real difficulty is created—certainly not because of any *deliberate* attempt to fit the complexities of political doctrines into too-tight categories, but because attention is directed toward the implications of the formal categories themselves. By in effect isolating the two kinds of doctrines from their broader theoretical contexts—at least as such contexts have developed in traditional political thought—a sharper opposition is presented than I believe has in fact existed, even at the level of theory. And by providing so sharp an opposition, the analysis is possibly deflected from the often subtle ways in which the problem has been treated, historically, by political theorists, jurists and theologians of various persuasions. In short, by the use of categories which tend to over-structure the theoretical dimension of the problem, the possibility of essentially different ways of perceiving that problem may be decreased.

My second point is that the abstract notion of a doctrine of *bellum justum* standing in opposition to a doctrine of reason of state is hard to reconcile with the way in which political leaders view the conduct of political affairs. One example here must suffice: During the second world war, Winston Churchill at one point argued for the mining of parts of the Norwegian coast in order to block Nazi shipments of ore to Germany. Churchill admitted that such an action would be a technical violation of a treaty with Norway. But he concluded that international law must, in this instance, give way temporarily to the consideration that England, as the leader at that time of the democratic nations, was fighting for the true cause of humanity.

Now it is true that, in the circumstances, England was fighting in all probability for her very existence as a free, independent political society. Even so, Churchill's appeal was not—at least not explicitly— to a right of mere survival, but to the quality of the political purposes or ends which he claimed England was fighting for. In any case, his arguments do not readily fit into either category of "doctrine." Nor is it at all easy to decide whether, in fact, the arguments he presents are his "real" reasons for advocating the action against Norway. Such a matter is always hard to decide in practice. For a decision must be based, I believe, on a careful examination of the character of the political leader, the regime he is part of, the attendant circumstances, and the actions which precede, accompany, and follow the advocacy. Furthermore, one cannot in advance exclude the possibility that such a man views the problem and its resolution in terms and in ways which simply defy categorization by rather formal categories. This does not mean that a critical observer is obliged to accept Churchill's or any other political actor's perceptions and attempted resolutions of these great problems of political conduct. But it does mean that a certain priority should go to a careful examination of the range and nature of the ways in which various political leaders have viewed such a problem, trying as hard as possible to stay within their notion of how to proceed.

III

To sum up: Just as categories may tend to over-structure the theoretical roots of a problem, so they may tend—and probably even more so than in the first case—to over-structure the political actor's ways of perceiving and reacting to actual political events. I grant that Tucker's purpose is not, as such, to consider either the detailed history of theoretical treatments in their contexts, or the detailed treatment of how specific political leaders view the problem of just war. And yet, I have had the feeling, from repeated reading of his paper, that the mode of treatment employed tends, willy-nilly, to deflect attention away from the problem as it appears in the realm of practice toward the problem as it can be treated by the prototypes of doctrines. In this respect, his general mode of treatment seems to me to be in tension with his own observation (f.n. 3) that all too rarely has the doctrine on either side really been examined in relation to practice. I would go further and suggest that the doctrines themselves need constantly to be viewed with respect to or in the light of the requirements of practice. For as I see the matter, theorizing about political conduct has to be guided by what practice requires. But what practice requires is by no means easily understood. And today, perhaps more than ever before, there is a widespread tendency to replace the effort to achieve such understanding with the effort to develop more sophisticated categories. Fortunately, Tucker, by his own repeated recognition that "certainty" of theoretical formulation is probably an impossible object, also redirects our attention to the prior problem of what practice requires. And yet, the formulation of the problem at the level of doctrine seems to me to cut across this endeavor.

TUCKER'S *BELLUM CONTRA BELLUM JUSTUM*

by Paul Ramsey

A statement of Jacques Maritain has recently become quite a consolation to me. "Moralists," he wrote in *Man and the State*, "are unhappy people. When they insist on the immutability of moral principles, they are reproached for imposing unlivable requirements on us. When they explain the way in which those immutable principles are to be put into force, they are reproached for making morality relative. In both cases, however, they are only upholding the claims of reason to direct life."

For which aspect of the professional work of a moralist Professor Tucker has the greater distaste, it is difficult to tell. Any attempt to show how moral principles work in political practice and in the conduct of war is like trying "to square the circle." The constituent elements of statecraft, Tucker believes, must revolve in a closed circle. The quest to define *legitimate* military necessity or *legitimate* reasons of state is bound, therefore, to eventuate either in the renunciation of statecraft or in the renunciation of morality.

Either of these contentions, taken alone, would be sufficient. It is interesting to note that Tucker thinks it worthwhile to undertake to prove both. Unless I misread him entirely, he is concerned to uphold not the necessities of statecraft alone, but the moral evil of these necessities. He writes about the state not like a seasoned and somewhat cynical practitioner of politics, but like a Socrates who himself would seek a private station and not a public one because of what he sees must be done for and by the state. Whenever some formulation of *bellum justum* threatens to become relevant to the ultimate safety of the state and of service to the political good, this must be demonstrated to have "emasculated the doctrine." The doctrine, it is insisted, must be square, lest the circle be successfully invaded or the statesman's task be illuminated by ethico-political insights that are not reduceable to the prudent wielding of quantitative increments of force in defense of the state.

Both Tucker and the pacifist insist that in statecraft—especially in the nuclear, deterrent state—evil must be done in order that good come of it. Tucker insists on this in behalf of the necessity of doing that evil when need be; the pacifist, in order to abandon statecraft. When the proponents of *bellum justum* attempt to cut down that evil by a proper political morality their undertaking is resisted by both as a betrayal of moral principles. The pacifist knows a lot about morality and what's evil; Tucker likewise knows very clearly what moral principles would be if there were any or any relevant to politics. Both also agree that to moralize the politics of the nation-state would mean to abandon its statecraft. This means that Tucker and the pacifist are in agreement as to the nature of "power politics." This is not surprising in an age when morality is a-political and politics is a-moral. Only Tucker is keener than most, in prosecuting this two-pronged objection to all attempts to "just-ify" force.

I

We will take up first the statement on modern war in the *Pastoral Constitution on the Church in the Modern World* issued by Vatican Council II, and Professor Tucker's comments on this.

The central declaration of the Vatican Council is its proscription as "a crime against God and man himself" of "any act of war aimed indiscriminately at the destruction of entire cities or extensive areas along with their population" (¶ 80). The fact that this is the most important statement of the Council is signalized by its use of the word "condemnation" this once among few if any other such usages in any of the sixteen promulgated Constitutions, Decrees, and Declarations, running to 103,000 words, issued by Vatican II. The Council did not even formally condemn atheism; yet, in language freely used at all previous councils but rarely by Vatican II, it condemns acts of war aimed indiscriminately at the destruction of entire cities with their populations.

Professor Tucker says that this prohibition is open to three possible interpretations, namely, that acts of war should not be aimed at the destruction of entire cities because this would (1) violate the moral immunity of noncombatants from direct attack, or (2) cause greater evil than any good resulting from such strikes, thus violating the principle of proportion, or (3) be tantamount to the "subjugation of peoples," and therefore in violation of the proscription of "aggressive" wars by recent Pontiffs even though the war had its origins in legitimate defense.

It seems obvious to me that the first is the only plausible reading. Either of the other explanations are strained. If the intention had been to condemn a certain kind of acts of modern war only because these actions would violate either the principle of proportion or the prohibition of aggression, the Council would have said simply *the destruction* of entire cities, etc. Instead it proscribes any act of war that is *aimed indiscriminately* at such destruction. This is another matter. The only reasonable explanation of the Council's choice of words is that this is *ordinary* language which expresses simply and forcefully what is meant by the more *technical* language of *bellum justum* enjoining the moral immunity of noncombatants from deliberate, direct attack.

Tucker himself remarks upon the "interesting, if not significant" omission of any express repetition of the recent denials that "aggressive" wars can possibly be just. Reference to this is not, as a matter of fact, lacking. The Council made "its own the condemnations of total war already pronounced by recent Popes," and that reference was enough, as it went on to introduce its own most solemn declaration. There are more references than this one.

Moreover, the second and third reasons are always *connected* in recent teachings: "aggressive" wars to restore violated rights, etc., cannot possibly be just *not* because wrongs should not be righted but because of the disproportionate evil that would be done in attempting to uproot an already established injustice, e.g., by wars of liberation.

Perhaps, as Tucker says, the Council considered this to be so evident as not to require lengthy reiteration either of the injustice of all aggressive wars, or of the ground for this judgment in disproportion (which, as a test, is everywhere expressed). In any case, if either or both of these explanations of the Council's central condemnation are correct, why did not the Council affirm this even more simply and directly instead of couching its meaning in the words ". . . aimed indiscriminately . . . "? Language forbidding aggressive wars and forbidding vast destruction that amounts to the same, while permitting just defense or permitting proportionate evil or permitting proportionate defense, has in recent years become quite customary in the Church's address to the problem of war and peace.

To explain why the Council invoked such familiar themes in the extraordinary language of its central condemnation would be far more difficult than to explain why, intending to invoke the rather complex doctrine of noncombatant immunity, it chose the simpler words ". . . aimed indiscriminately . . ." for a new emphasis it wanted to introduce into the Church's guidance of men in the face of modern war.

If this is correct, Tucker asks, "Why did the Council not affirm the rights of the innocent even more simply and directly by stating in traditional terms the principle of noncombatant immunity from direct attack?" The answer to that question is that such language is *not* familiar. It is rather the technical language of moral theology, and this is a pastoral constitution addressed to all mankind in which it was proper to use other language for the same idea. If even Tucker has not yet rightly grasped the meaning of the moral immunity of non-combatants from direct attack as this is comprehended in moral science, the Council is rather to be commended for simply declaring that it is most wicked to aim indiscriminately at the destruction of entire cities or extensive areas along with their population.

The point here is quite clear. For there to be any capital "crime," not only in the legal order, but the "crime against God and man" of which the Council speaks, there must be *mens rea* as well as the objectively evil deed. It is not a sin or crime without both: not only the destruction, the disproportion, not only the subjugation or anni-hilation of great numbers among the adversary, but also *the aiming of* acts of war *indiscriminately* upon entire cities.

Moreover, not only had the Council in many other paragraphs directed attention to the grave danger that any modern war will do greater evil than the evil it prevents or the good it secures (the prin-ciple of proportion). It has also *not* neglected to repeat in the clearest possible terms the recent Papal teachings limiting just war to legiti-mate defense and calling attention to the danger that war begun in defense may, because of the nature of modern scientific weapons, easily become in the objective order tantamount to the prohibited aggression. "It is one thing to undertake military action for the just defense of the people, and something else again to seek the subjuga-tion of other nations" (¶ 79), the Council pronounced in *principle*. Then it remarked as a matter of *fact* that "acts of war involving these weapons can inflict massive and indiscriminate destruction far exceed-ing the bounds of legitimate defense" (¶ 80). It is not reasonable to suppose that in the Council's central condemnation it chose more obscure language to express something said more clearly in other paragraphs; or that it introduced the reference to aiming indiscrim-inately at the destruction of entire cities and areas along with their population in order to say no more than that this destruction as such would be excessive or beyond the limits of just defense or both. Instead, we have to conclude that the Council chose less obscure, more familiar and less technical language to express the principle of discrimination than the language in which moral theologians usually analyse the meaning of this principle and justify and explain it in terms of the moral immunity of noncombatants from direct attack.

70

The language was well chosen also because it enabled the Council at one and the same time to direct attention to the "central war" now planned and designed by the nuclear powers as a consequence of applying in statecraft only the constituent element of responding to the threat and use of force by quantitative increments of the same threats and force. To have approached the overriding issue facing today's world by first of all expressing the principle of discrimination in terms of the general moral argument for the immunity of non-combatants from direct attack would have focused attention upon any and all comparatively minor acts of wrongdoing in war, and not upon where the abomination is most clearly to be found. This Tucker seems to demand of the Council when he lays down the requirement that we be told "the *acts* that are absolutely forbidden"—or else he proposes to run away with the conclusion that the Council came instead to a "near emasculation of this immunity" in what it said about "entire cities" and "extensive areas" (p. 45).

I agree with Professor Tucker that in its analysis of deterrence and the morality of deterrence the Council leaves standing the assumption that we may intend to do evil that good may come (f.n. 34). But in the matter of the actual conduct of war the Council has clearly declared, in its "unequivocal and unhesitating condemnation" of "acts of war that aim indiscriminately at the destruction of entire cities," that the nations ought never, in the actual prosecution of war itself, to do evil that good may come. Perhaps the Council should have said that deterrent postures that rest upon aiming indiscriminately at entire cities, if this requires that we make ourselves conditionally willing to go to such acts of war, are equally to be condemned. Then it would have made a beginning toward a fuller analysis of the morality of deterrence. But then I fail to see why Professor Tucker thinks it important to direct against the analysis of the morality of deterrence which I have proposed not so much the objection that this would mean the renunciation of statecraft as the objection that I too have emasculated the doctrine as such and (quoting, significantly, a Catholic pacifist) "abused" double-effect categories in using them (p. 37; n. 26). Apparently, a moralist must remain as "square" as the Council is silent on the morality of deterrence lest the nature and valid requirements of statecraft be addressed relevantly.[1]

The most revealing encounter between Tucker's position and the

---

[1] See also my article "The Vatican Council and Modern Warfare," published concurrently in *Theological Studies*, June, 1966, and in *Theology Today*, July, 1966.

Council document takes place in a fairly obscure footnote (p. 45; n. 32). Here we find his premises disclosing themselves as premises and not arguments. The Council's central declaration, he writes, "leaves open the possibility that any act of war 'aimed discriminately at the destruction of entire cities' may not be forbidden, unless, of course, the destruction of cities is, by definition, an indiscriminate act." Then, Tucker continues, the statement would be "simply redundant rather than ambiguous. Instead it should read: 'any act of war aimed at the destruction of entire cities . . . is indiscriminate and is a crime against God and man himself.'"

Of course, the prohibition of any act of war aimed indiscriminately at the destruction of entire cities leaves open possibilities which the Council does not address, such as the possibility that the destruction of an entire city may be the consequence of a discriminating act of war. It is Professor Tucker, and not the Council, who in the main would deduce the intention of an act of war, its aim and its moral quality, backward, as it were, from the destruction wrought. One might frame for the Council a statement that verbally begins with a sweeping condemnation of the physical destruction of entire cities, like the one of Pope Pius XII condemning modern war unless, of course, this could be in self-defense. The reformulation would read: "An act of war that destroys entire cities or extensive areas along with their populations is a crime against God and man himself, unless of course such acts are or could be aimed discriminately at the destruction of proper military targets."

In no case, however, is the Council's most solemn declaration either redundant or ambiguous. It cannot be reduced to a sort of *synthetic apriori* or synthetic redundancy which merely hold that the physical destruction of cities is by definition an indiscriminate act. Neither is it to be reduced to a logically analytic redundancy which merely announces that an indiscriminate act is by definition forbidden because it is indiscriminate. After all, quantitative economy in the use of force is able to prohibit wanton, indiscriminate destruction of cities in war (unless, of course, the destruction could be prudent or proportionate to the ends in view). Instead, the words "aimed indiscriminately" plainly rest the validity of the condemnation upon the prior category of murder and upon distinguishing this from indirect, unintended, killing in war which is not aimed at. At the same time, the words "the destruction of entire cities and of extensive areas along with their population" lay hold on and encompass what may be the central plan and design of modern war. It thus proposes to be an ethico-political statement about proper and improper conduct of statecraft, and one that shows the immediate relevance of a rock-bottom moral principle to the determination of the constituent elements of legitimate or illegitimate appeals to military necessity. As such, the Council's most solemn declaration has to be faced and endorsed or disapproved by political consciences.

II

In any discussion of the claims of reason to direct statecraft, against or in modification of the claims of necessity, it is of first importance to distinguish the unchanging principles which govern the use of force from the practice which these principles (if there are any) require from age to age because of the changing shape of warfare.

The objective of combat is the incapacitation of a combatant from doing what he is doing because he is this particular combatant in this particular war; it is *not* the killing of a man because he is a man or because he is this particular man. The latter and only the latter would be "murder." This is the indestructable difference between murder and killing in war; and the difference is to be found in the intention and direction of the action that kills. From the requirement that just acts of war be directed upon the combatant and not upon the man flows the prohibition of the killing of soldiers who by surrender have taken themselves out of the war and incapacitated themselves from continuing it. The men are not to be killed when effective combatancy is no longer in them, since all along it was the combatant and not the man who had to be stopped.

From this also flows the cardinal principle governing just conduct in war, namely the moral immunity of noncombatants from deliberate, direct attack. This is the principle of *discrimination,* and in it there are two ingredients. One is the prohibition of "deliberate, direct attack." This is the immutable, unchanging ingredient in the definition of justice in war. In order to get to know the meaning of "aiming discriminately" *vs.* "aiming *in*discriminately," one has only to pay attention to the nature of an action and analyse action in a proper fashion. The second ingredient is the meaning of "combatancy-noncombatancy." This is relativistic and varying in meaning and application. As Tucker says, "combatancy-noncombatancy" is a function of how the nations and their forces are organized for war, and it is in some measure a function of military technology. In this he is as correct as, we shall see, he is mistaken when in the same fashion he seeks to fix the meaning of "deliberate, direct attack."

There are at least three constituent elements in the moral life and in any ethical analysis of morality. There are first the *motives* of the agent and any other ingredients that may, so to speak, be in his head or in his subjective consciousness. There is secondly the *intention* of his action. And there is thirdly the ultimate ends or consequences of the action. Each of these has to be reckoned in a complete appraisal of morality. While the terms moralists use vary, ordinarily *goodness* or its opposite are said to characterize the motives of agents; *right* or *wrong*, the intended shape of the action; and *good* or *evil*, the ultimate effects.

Since the moral immunity of noncombatants from direct attack is a doctrine that rests upon an analysis of the intentionality of actions of a military sort, the *pons asinorum* for understanding the meaning of this requires that the intention of the action be always distinguished from the motives of men (and from anything else that may be in their heads besides intentional aims) and from the final, expected consequences of the course of events set going by those actions. Any collapse of these elements into one another will be a mistake. This is what accounts for most of the gross misunderstandings of what is even proposed by proponents of the principle of discrimination in the political use of violence. This also accounts for Tucker's evident misreading of the meaning of right conduct in *bellum justum*.

Tucker seems to agree that the subjective motives of men should be largely set aside in trying to penetrate the meaning of *just conduct* in war. He says that subjective consciousness is too "indeterminate," by which I judge he means that motives and the subjective states of agents are too various and variable to be of much help in determining the meaning of just conduct or of prudent conduct in politics and in military strategy. This is correct, however important the motives of men are in character analysis and even if moral motives and character are not without significance in the conduct of affairs.

Presumably the death of combatants ideally should not be *wanted*. *Wanting* the death that is done to combatants and *not wanting* the death done to noncombatants cannot, then, be the meaning of the principle of discrimination surrounding the latter with moral immunity from direct attack in war. Still Tucker fails to maintain this distinction between whatever else may be in the heads of human agents and the intention of their actions, and between the intention of an action and its ultimate consequences.

He collapses *foreknowledge* of unavoidable death and damage to civilians collateral to the destruction of legitimate military targets into the meaning of *intending* or meaning to kill them. Anything I *knew* would happen must be an undifferentiated part of the meaning of what I meant or intended to do. This is simply a flaw in ethical analysis that cannot withstand examination. If motives such as hatred or subjectively wanting or not wanting the killing are not decisive in determining the intention of the action, neither is knowledge of the attendant results along with the intended results sufficient to obliterate a significant moral and political distinction between these two sorts of immediate effects of all acts of war. Indeed, in one important respect Professor Tucker's language is not apt or technical enough to lead him to a right understanding of this teaching in the theory of *bellum justum*. He correctly speaks of *direct* and *indirect action*. But then he speaks in parallel fashion of *directly* or *indirectly intending* something, where the doctrine speaks instead of intending or *not* intending something. The deaths of noncombatants are to be only *indirectly done* and they should be *un*intended in the just conduct of war whose actions may and should be, and are intended to be, directed upon combatants and legitimate military objectives. This aiming of intention and of action is entirely compatible with *certain* knowledge that a great number of civilian lives will unintendedly be indirectly destroyed. (Both are quite different from *wanting* either from malicious motives.)

Thus, Professor Tucker deduces the intention of an act of war from the consequences that are foreseen. In fact, he is inclined to deduce intention from the nature and objective amount of the destruction done. When this latter step has been taken, the excellent start that was made by distinguishing between wanting and intending something remains in the words only, and is of little usefulness in the analysis of military plans and actions. Because Professor Tucker finally believes that intention is as indeterminate and variable as motive, he rightly locates motives in the hearts of men where they have no immediate significance in analyzing statecraft or acts of war, and he wrongly deduces or determines the intentions of political agents and of military actions by reference to events in the objective order alone. Between the motives of men and the total consequences of their actions, the meaning of intention is squeezed out.

This simply makes it impossible for Tucker to grasp the meaning of "aiming indiscriminately," or the meaning of the intention. Thus the actual aiming and the actual or the foreseen destruction are telescoped together, or at least the meaning of the intention is given by the destruction foreseen. But since he wishes to retain the word "intention," and wishes to use it in political analysis at least to refute *bellum justum*, he gives it a meaning it never had in that theory.

In only extreme cases will it appear to be proper to move from events in the objective order to the attribution of intentions to agents or to their actions. If I use a sledge hammer to kill a fly on my neighbor's bald head it may be not unreasonably supposed that I had a grudge against my neighbor in my motives and also that by my action I *meant* (intended, "aimed") to do him harm. This might be called getting bonus-neighbor-damage while prosecuting man's war against the insects, if indeed killing the fly was not itself incidental to the aiming of my destructive act upon his head. Similarly, from the extensive destruction of Dresden, from the cruciality of the vast firestorm to the plan of attack (to light the way for successive waves of bombers), it is not unreasonable to conclude that the destruction of the railway complex was incidental, even if we had no other evidence for the fact the railway complex was not even aimed at.

In general, it simply has to be said that these days we are better able to analyze play-acting than moral action. We speak of the "intention" of a drama as something in the play, in the action itself, not to be identified with everything the author thought he was writing. Similarly, the intention of a human action cannot be identified with everything the author thought or knew, or thought he knew, about the total consequences. Beginning in the *aiming* of the action, the intention of an act then includes the main *thrust* of it upon its immediate objective. There is, thus, a distinction between what is directly done by the thrust of action and what is incidentally, indirectly done attendant upon this thrust. Only the immediate objective is subjectively intended; the other foreseeable effects are *un*intended.

This brings us to the need to distinguish the intention of the act and its immediate effects from the ultimate consequences. The intention or thrust of the action is by no means directed immediately toward ultimate consequences, but toward the production of an immediate event that is reasonably believed itself to be productive of those future good consequences. Professor Tucker magnifies the doing of evil that good may come, first, by falsely implying that everything foreseeably done in the event was in some sense intended and then, secondly, by lumping everything done in the event (including collateral civilian deaths) without differentiation into the "means" by which politically good consequences are obtained. This too is a mistake in the analysis of action.

Perhaps an illustration will demonstrate more clearly what is at stake in distinguishing between the immediate effects of action (some intended and direct, others unintended and indirect) from the ultimate good consequences an action seeks to serve. The intention or present thrust of action concerns immediate effects, not the ulterior purposes or objectives. The latter may be *good* and yet the intention be *wrong*. Indeed in some respects it would be more correct to say that the motives of men rather than their intentions are oriented upon ultimate objectives. While granting that this may only be a verbal convention, it has at least to be said that the "intention" of which *bellum justum* speaks is not fixed on ultimate ends. Perhaps we need to change the convention and speak of intention in two different senses. There would be intention 1 to indicate the usage of this word in *bellum justum*. Then there is intention 2 to indicate the meaning Tucker gives to this word. But this is certain: Tucker's meaning cannot be used to interpret the meaning this word has in *bellum justum*, or to refute that theory by proving it ambiguous. It can only be used to displace it, and thus to instate another understanding of morality or of statecraft, or both. Before coming fully to grips with Tucker's displacing definition, I will stick with the convention, and ask:

What is at stake in not collapsing the intention of human actions into orientation upon the ends produced?

Take the case of mortal conflict between the life of a mother and her unborn child. It is well known that Roman Catholic teaching prohibits, in this conflict between equals, *direct* abortion as a means of saving the mother's life. Suppose someone wants to contend against this verdict and to justify *direct* abortion in such cases. Unless he denies the premise that the unborn child is a human being, it will not be sufficient for him simply to *assert* arbitrarily that direct abortion is the right action because this will save the life of the mother. The goodness of this ultimate result was never in question. No one doubts that the proposed medical action will respect the sanctity of the mother's life. The question that was raised is whether direct abortion is not in every way incompatible with any remaining regard for the sanctity of the nascent life.

In order for anyone to wrestle with his Catholic brother over the verdict forbidding direct abortion, he will have to propose another penetration of the intention and main thrust of this action and its immediate effects. He will have to say something significantly different from the Catholic view about direct abortion *as an action brought upon the child*. If instead he prattles endlessly about saving the mother's life he shows only that he does not know where the argument is, since that ultimate good was never in question. It helps not at all to say that we should do what a charitable reason requires in the final consequence, since the question is whether every shred of respect for the sanctity of nascent life must not be abandoned ever to do such a thing (direct killing of the innocent) for the sake of those consequences. No one ever doubted that the proposed action has effects that are ultimately charitable to the mother. It is therefore no argument to say that it is. The issue to be faced is whether the present action demonstrates (in its intention and in the shape of its primary thrust in the world and in its immediate effects) any remaining recognition of the fact that the littlest and least important human life has a sanctity that is not wholly to be denied in anything we now do.

This is precisely the issue raised by proponents of the moral immunity of noncombatants from direct attack (or, more briefly, the principle of discrimination) as a principle that should govern the political use of violence. It is no answer to affirm that there are ultimate ends which statecraft must have in view, even the preservation of a just or humane political order as a safe dwelling place for the human beings remaining alive and for future generations of men all of whom have a dignity and sanctity which should be respected. It is not enough simply to reiterate that this is a good and proper end of politics, with the implication, without argument, that to this all else is properly menial. The question that was raised was how the ends of the state can be served by plans and acts of war that evidence some remaining respect for the sanctity of persons now alive and with whom we are presently engaged. The proposal was that, if one focuses attention upon the intention and thrust of present action, it will be evident that acts of war *aimed indiscriminately* at the destruction of entire cities and extensive areas along with their populations cannot possibly be compatible with any remaining regard for the sanctity of human life as such. The contention is that if one is going to justify killing in war this must be intentionally limited (in the sense explained) to combatants and to the destruction of legitimate military objectives, and that one's just regard for the dignity of manhood and one's resolve not to reduce this to a mere instrument of statecraft will manifest itself in noncombatant immunity as a regulative principle. It is no answer to this argument to proceed to collapse the intention of present action into the ultimate ends of statecraft, the goodness of which no proponent of *bellum justum* ever meant to question. What would be required, in order to refute the traditional understanding of just conduct in war, would be another penetration of the present intention and thrust of acts of war and their immediate effects that seeks to show that noncombatant immunity or the principle of discrimination does not adequately express the justice governing present action and intention. What is required would be a reforming and not a displacing definition of intention. I venture to believe that such a properly targeted rebuttal cannot succeed.

III

Professor Tucker is quite correct in saying that it is only when we come to the means permitted in warfare that we find "a significant conflict between the necessities of the state [as he conceives these] and the demands of *bellum justum*" (p. 21). He is led somewhat astray by his use of the word "means." "Means" are not right or wrong. Only "conduct" is: the conduct or "the manner of warfare."

There are two principles governing the conduct of war: proportion and discrimination. The principle of discrimination forbidding deliberate, direct attack upon whole cities and areas with their population apparently opens up the greater gulf between necessity of state and the requirements of political morality. Still this begins to be the case with regard to the principle of proportion. Let us look first at what Tucker says about this, and ask whether he has in this connection properly located the beginning of a difference between *bellum justum* and his own view of statecraft.

Professor Tucker writes (p. 18) that a "proportionality of effectiveness" is permitted in international law. This means economy in the use of force, or the proportioning of means of violence to the effective protection of endangered interests or values. This he contrasts with a "proportionality of value" which he says characterizes *bellum justum*. This, I take it, means not only proportioning means to ends along the single track of protecting the *endangered* interests or values. It means taking account of other values as well. Since the use of force not only protects values but must pay costs in other values, the values preserved need to be proportioned to the values sacrificed through the use of force. Whatever be the meaning of the permissions and requirements of international law, it seems clear that the requirements of a realistic statecraft and the requirements of *bellum justum* must be in agreement in this respect. Surely, both the conduct of statecraft and the just conduct of war enjoin not only the use of the force and no more than the force needed effectively to protect endangered values, but also the reckoning of those values against the values that will be destroyed in the course of that same use of force. The principle of proportion, in short, is no more than a counsel of political prudence. One should not only use effective force and no more than that. One ought also to count the costs of doing this (even effectively doing this), and weigh all the cost/benefits.

Admittedly, this justification of and limitation upon the use of force does not tell the statesman what to do. It leaves this for him to decide by virtue of political prudence. It is precisely a worth of the principle of proportion that this enables no man to bring against statecraft an extrinsic norm. But this is not to agree with the charge that "a prescription the converse of which is manifestly absurd can tell us very little that is meaningful about how men ought to behave." Tucker seems to regard this as a weakness in the "proportionality of value." This means no more than sound statecraft counting all the costs/benefits as well as effectiveness in protecting the values that were threatened. Such counsels of prudence are by no means useless because their converse (Be imprudent! Pay more costs than the benefits are worth!) is manifestly absurd. Moreover, a "proportionality of effectiveness" is likewise a prescription the converse of which is manifestly absurd. The worth of these propositions, or of the use of them in analyzing sound statecraft and justice in the political use of violence, stems from the fact that men and statesmen very often do things that are manifestly absurd, led on by rhetoric, bravado, and inflexible postures. Moreover, a "proportionality of effectiveness" is no more informative. When Churchill made the decision to stand against Nazi Germany he could not then have known that a few months later Hitler would make the stupid mistake (fighting on two fronts by his attack upon Russia) which proved Churchill's decision to have been a politically prudent one. He could not have known this whether the standard he consulted was that of a realistic statecraft (national self-interest, defending the "self" and independence of the state, or a proportionality of effectiveness alone) or whether the standard was a broader conception of the common good (counting all the cost/benefits according to a proportionality of value). Tucker's campaign against the *bellum justum,* and in this instance against its proportionality of value because it is "devoid of substantive content" (p. 18; n. 13), is carried so far that it must turn against his own conception of one of the constituent elements of statecraft.

However, it may be that by "proportionality of value" Tucker means, in a somewhat inept choice of words, to refer to taking into account more than one's own national good in the calculation of cost/benefits that would justify or forbid resort to arms. If so, then a proportionality of value would be different from the proportionality of effectiveness governing the conduct of a narrow statecraft and enshrined in international law. It is true that *bellum justum* requires of political prudence not only a calculus of all the values paid but also of the values exacted, even of an adversary. It envisions an international system which, while properly described as a state of war, ought not to be termed a non-moral state of nature.

Therefore, justice in the conduct of war, even the prudent conduct of war, meant some reference to harmonizing the national common good to the common good of all men and nations. I suspect that the traditional principle of proportion always assumed that there might be some costs too great, even when exacted of an adversary, to be worth the value protected on one's own part or for the good and safety of one's own state. The present writer does not believe, any more than Tucker does, that there are any "wandering nations" which, like our father Abraham, are called or answer the call to go out from the integrity of their selfhood into a far country which they know not. But short of this, there is an inclusion of the values of other peoples as well as the values of one's own which *bellum justum* seeks to acknowledge in international relations even when there is war. The nation is not *the absolute* even if none is Abraham. Perhaps Tucker has not made enough of the difference between his own view of statecraft and that contained in *bellum justum* which begins to emerge here even in the meaning and application of the principle of proportion in justifying or forbidding political resort to violence.

In turning from proportion to discrimination in assessing justice in the conduct of war, we need to note that these are different tests but that both are always needed in determining the justice of warfare. One test without the other, or one instead of the other, can never lead to the verdict: this is justifiable to do. We also need to note that, of the two, the principle of proportion or political prudence provides, in face of the destructiveness of modern warfare, the greatest pressure toward redefining *jus contra bellum*. This has been a parallel development in international law and in *bellum justum* (vide: modern Papal teachings). But the stress on limiting "the manner of warfare" by forbidding acts of war aimed indiscriminately at noncombatants and combatants alike has been to the point of defining *jus in bello,* not to enforcing *jus ad bellum* or *jus contra bellum*. This is so much the case that one of Professor Tucker's main objections to the principle of discrimination proscribing direct attack upon noncombatants in the conduct of war, strangely, seems to be that this test, taken alone, allows for a far higher level of violence in legitimate riposts than are prudent today or proportionate. Only he does not seem to know that this principle of discrimination is not to be taken alone. Nor should he imply that anyone must be either stupid or morally insensitive who says that a certain plan of war, e.g., tactical nuclear war or counterinsurgency war, as the nations are presently organized for war, might be a quite discriminating plan of war, while the destructiveness of it may or may not be a disproportionate cost to pay or exact for the political goods at stake. There are two *connected* principles.

81

Tucker is altogether correct, however, in resisting the reduction of the principle of discrimination to "in effect, another form of calculation." There are *two* principles.

> it is not enough to argue that one may never do evil that good may come because the good will not come (only the evil),[2] or that the evil act will corrupt the actor and thereby defeat his ends . . ., or that the means cannot be separated from the ends but are themselves the ends in the very process of coming into existence. . . . If certain means are to be absolutely forbidden they must be forbidden quite apart from these considerations. If certain means are to be absolutely forbidden they must be forbidden because of their intrinsic evil. If one may never do evil that good may come, it is not—or not primarily—because the good will not come but simply because one may never do evil (p. 22).

Professor Tucker is also quite correct in ascribing to the theory of *bellum justum*, at the point of gravest potential conflict with "reasons of state" which he identifies, the implied verdict that "the state cannot be considered a supreme value for men" and also (if the state is instrumental to other values) the verdict that those values which "the state, and perhaps only the state, may serve to protect also cannot be considered supreme" (p. 23). It is, indeed, because and only because human lives possess a dignity and value which transcends the state and all the values the state serves to protect that, in the service of the state and in the exercise of statecraft, there are limits to those individuals who may be deliberately made the objects of attack in war.

Finally one can grant that "it is only where the prohibition against the deliberate killing of noncombatants is considered absolute that a clear conflict *may arise* between the necessities of the state and the requirements of an ethic which presumably sets limits to those necessities" (p. 24; italics added). This possible conflict, however, has to be *proved*. A political ethic that "sets limits" to the exercise of statecraft does not therefore go *contrary* to the vital interests of the state. It may only indicate among its necessities its choice-

---

[2] We should note, however, at this point that the moral judgment "it is never right to do wrong that good may come" is neither withdrawn nor weakened by referring anyone who argues that this would call for the abandonment of statecraft to the footnote the nuclear age has written to this perennial truth: "it can never do any good to do wrong that good may come of it." The latter simply affirms the compatibility of morality with statecraft. "Acts of war aimed indiscriminately at the destruction of entire cities . . . are a crime against God and man himself" is not a true ethico-political statement *because* it is also the case that such a war would be self-defeating statecraft. Morality may be prudent without being moral because it is prudent.

82

worthy necessities (and even Tucker's necessities of state are "necessities" for choice).

IV

It is time now to grapple more closely with Tucker's displacing definition of the intention that governs the meaning of noncombatant immunity from direct attack. At the outset it should be clearly stated that he is quite at liberty himself to hold his particular understanding of intention. Such a view of the intentionality of acts of war would then be entirely consistent with the necessities of state-craft as Tucker conceives these to be, since it is in fact drawn forth from this understanding. His interpretation could then be used to *assert* the *irrelevance* of *bellum justum*. The latter and "reasons of state" would simply be squared off in opposition to one another as doctrines of state: abandon justice all ye who enter statecraft; abandon statecraft all who seek to act justly in politics and in military affairs.

But Tucker's displacing definition cannot be used to show the emasculation of the theory of *bellum justum* by its proponents, since plainly it is he who holds this understanding of it, and not they. I confess that this interpretation of the issue posed by Tucker may be fairer to its author than a reader may suppose to be substantiated by a first reading of his essay. Most of the time Tucker *does* seem to be offering *an interpretation* of the meaning of noncombatant immunity and of the intention entailed in direct attack proposed by *bellum justum*. He *does* seem to be proposing an explanatory or even reforming definition (one that better states the meaning of the theory itself) and not a displacing one. If this is the correct reading, then, Tucker's account of the doctrine is simply a mistake he has made while doing political philosophy.

He begins auspiciously and comes close to rightly apprehending the meaning; yet in the end he drives to a point most remote from it. He begins auspiciously, by noting that in "the moral immunity of noncombatants from deliberate, direct attack" there are two concepts in need of separate definition. This opened the way toward an affirmation that "noncombatancy" when correctly understood indicates how the principle of discrimination can be relatively and variably applied in the practice of war, while "deliberate, direct attack" when correctly understood indicates the unchanging element in the principle. At once, however, both these features of the definition of the immunity, and not only the meaning of noncombatancy, are defined by Professor Tucker by reference to objective events in the world or the objective

83

destruction brought about by acts of war. Thus he barred himself from an understanding of "aiming indiscriminately."

Still he does begin auspiciously by clearly defending the fitness of the notion of noncombatancy in the direction of war's conduct. We should follow him in this, and not the ordinary critics of *bellum justum*.

Who are the "innocent" who are not to be deliberately attacked?

Tucker answers this question with a categorical statement that "unless the very concept of noncombatant status is itself suppressed," the difficulties over the precise characteristics requisite for this status "are not likely to prove intractable" (p. 25). If, as he remarks in a footnote at this point, the distinction "is far more relative and pragmatic in application than is commonly admitted," proponents of *bellum justum* should be among the first to admit this. There can be no reason for anyone to resist the notion that combatancy-noncombatancy has been and will continue to be "dependent both on the manner in which states organize for war and on the technology with which they conduct war." Only a legalist-pacifist employment of the *bellum justum* doctrine would think of supposing otherwise, in the hope of bringing peace by discrediting one by one all wars, or all modern war. Since *bellum justum* proposes to indicate to statesmen how within tolerable moral limits they may make use of violence in the preservation of the state's politically embodied justice and in defense of its "self" and independence, how could it be otherwise than that this distinction governing just conduct in war should be relative to the shape of war in any period Not Yet the Plowshares? This being so, I fail to see why Tucker later on waxes so eloquent in condemning the seeming moral insensibility of my defense of the possible justice (so far as noncombatant immunity alone is concerned) of counter-force nuclear strikes in an age when there are military establishments fifty or more miles in diameter and legitimate targets deeply buried.[3]

---

[3] Again, it is not discrimination defining *jus in bello,* but prudence or proportion transforming *jus ad bellum* into *jus contra bellum* in the face of the destructiveness of modern war that imposes the more severe limits upon the state's use of violent means. This calls for radical revision of Tucker's judgment that there is an irrepressible conflict between *jus in bello* and necessities of state. The more severe limitation upon statecraft will already have arisen from a principle that is undeniably inherent in its proper exercise, namely, prudence or proportion. Moreover, the principle of proportion is controlling over the principle of discrimination in determining whether it is finally *just to do* even those actions in war that can be shown to be discriminate. Thus, Tucker is entirely mistaken in saying that any proponent of *bellum justum* would contend that the

Moreover, to argue that noncombatancy is, unlike subjective inno-cence, susceptible to "objective determination" is not to argue that it is susceptible to *certain* determination. True enough, the determina-tion of noncombatancy depends upon the "subjective appreciation" of what constitutes this status in one or another organization for war, on the part of our political leaders and citizens alike in public delib-eration. But one is not concerned with the subjective appreciation of something that is itself subjective, namely, guilt or innocence. It was surely a gratuitous remark (and one that may indicate that Tucker scarcely appreciates the fact that *bellum justum* is a doctrine of state-craft, for statesmen, to be determined in its application by statesmen) for him to write: "In the subjective interpretation of this behavior [constituting noncombatancy] there is no apparent reason for ac-cording greater weight to the insights of Christian moralists than to the insights of others" (p. 25; n. 19). Of course not!

What is the meaning of deliberate attack upon noncombatants?

This, Professor Tucker rightly says, is the question that "pose[s] very considerable difficulties"—far more difficulties than the question of who are, or whether there are any, noncombatants—and he then proceeds to demonstrate that he himself has not yet surmounted the main difficulty he points out in understanding the meaning of this immunity. He asserts summarily, and without an attempt at demon-stration by a careful analysis of the meaning of "direct" and "indirect" attack, that the qualification of the prohibition of direct attack by the permission of collateral noncombatant destruction (or some instances of this qualification) is "to be explained in terms of military neces-sity. . . . The scope afforded to the principle of noncombatant im-munity has always been dependent upon the scope afforded to military necessity" (p. 26). Thus the prohibition of deliberate attack upon non-combatants really means that belligerents may take those measures required for the success of their military operations unless these are forbidden by one or another positive law of war.

What seemed to be introduced was an endeavor to render tract-

---

evil effects of counter-force nuclear strikes, "whatever might be said of their proportionality or disproportionality, would still not be the doing of evil" (p. 32). Knowingly to do a disproportionate act is wicked (since prudence is a virtue), even on the excuse that only legitimate targets are attacked. Note 26 to p. 37 contains a more accurate statement of the case: "Even if we were to accept the view that the 'indirect effect' of killing half a population would not be the doing of evil [read: "would not be indiscriminate," since there are two tests of the evil.] there would still remain the question of the proportionality of the action."

able the very considerable difficulties in the way of understanding the meaning of "deliberate attack." This trial ends, in the very same paragraph, with an essay on the vagaries of men or the history of injustice in war (only we cannot tell this unless first the meaning of direct attack has been fully understood). Let it be said that this notion is better expressed on p. 28.[4] But here at the outset Professor Tucker has introduced his theme: noncombatant immunity from direct attack (not only "noncombatancy" but "direct attack" as well) must derive its meaning in one way or another from what is done in the objective order. Damage done that was foreseeable, for example, must have been "intended."

"Noncombatancy" is a category whose meaning varies from age to age according to military technology and the way nations are organized for war. But "direct" or "deliberate attack" in the statement of the immunity is not relative. This means, of course, that the meaning of the immunity varies *in its application* from age to age; but not that the meaning of deliberate, direct attack is a relative matter. The reason for this is that the concept of "direct attack" gives the shape to *an action* (its intention and thrust) while "noncombatancy" is a function of the bare facts of military organization.

Tucker argues from the admitted relativity of noncombatancy as a category to the relativity of "deliberate, direct attack" as a category. This is a mistake.

His misstep is plainly evident from the topic he takes up immediately after having introduced, as a separate question, the meaning of "direct attack," and the unsupported assertions about this that we have cited above. On p. 26 we find ourselves dealing with "the concept of military objective." Surely this is a return to the first question (pp. 24–25) concerning noncombatancy. At least, a discussion of the meaning of "military objective" is far closer to a further probing of

---

[4] This more adequate comprehension of the meaning of the intention and direction of action is, however, promptly confused again by the unsupported assertions that *bellum justum* "for the most part . . . deduces intent from these consequences," "by inquiry into the character of the means he has chosen." In the next sentence, the correct approach again emerges: "The character of the means . . . is in turn determined by inquiry into *the action itself*"—only to be buried again by the words: "above all by inquiry into the *consequences* that might have been reasonably expected to follow from the action" (pp. 28–29; italics added). In Section II above, I attempted to set down an account of "intention" that is apt to unpack the confusion in these expressions, and correct them—on the assumption that Professor Tucker meant to offer us a reforming or interpretative definition and not merely his own displacement of the traditional meaning.

the meaning of combatancy than it is to being an extension or further grappling with the problem of the meaning of deliberate attack, concerning which there were "very considerable difficulties" to subdue. Tucker first analyzed the meaning of the immunity into the two questions, concerning noncombatancy and concerning deliberate attack. This is the only fruitful approach. But then he collapsed these categories again without having probed deeply enough the meaning of "deliberate attack" which steadfastly governs the meaning of the immunity and of just *conduct* in war.

In any case there is no reason to disagree that the nature of a military objective is a function of the manner in which societies organize for war. This is the "same dependence" the category of noncombatancy was allowed to have. But the same dependency is nowhere proved to pertain to the meaning of deliberate, direct attack.

Of course it is the case—taking the immunity as a whole, in both its crucial aspects—"that the scope of the immunity accorded the civilian population is largely dependent upon the meaning given the concept of military objective and that the concept of military objective varies with the character of war" (p. 26). This only means that *bellum justum* is a doctrine of statecraft. It proposes to tell the statesman how, even in war, reason can direct life (as Maritain put it). But in no way does Tucker demonstrate his assertion that the meaning properly to be given to military objective depends on the meaning given by military necessity, or that the meaning of the intentional aim can be inferred from the scope of the destruction.

Apart from the semblances of plausibility (p. 27) that have their explanation in the vagaries and pretensions of men in the fog and fury of war, there are only three ways to accomplish this reduction of the meaning of noncombatant immunity to the scope of military necessity. One way would be to show that noncombatancy (and military objective) as a category is quite indeterminate. A second way would be to demonstrate that in some past or present organization for war everyone in a society is a fighter without any distinctions of degrees of remoteness or proximity to its military power. Professor Tucker does not undertake to show either of these two things to be the case. Indeed, he affirms that a definition of noncombatancy is tractable. The remaining way would be to show, by a careful examination of the meaning of "deliberate, direct attack" as a rule of practice specifying the meaning of just and unjust conduct, that this in principle does actually depend upon the variable meanings given to the concept of military necessity. Perhaps the reason Professor Tucker does not undertake to probe the meaning of direct attack so deeply is that he knows that this will prove the opposite. For here we come upon the "immutable principle" for which the admittedly variable meanings of "noncombatancy" and "military objective" show the application—producing the concept of *legitimate* military necessity.

Tucker's cardinal assertions have no weight, if he meant to give us an interpretation of *bellum justum*, and not his own view of statecraft in another guise. "Whether the death and injury done to the innocent is directly intended or is beside the intention of the actor is *determined by the scope of this death and injury*." That is a palpably false account of the doctrine of just conduct. Given this false account, *of course* how much death and injury will be regarded as violating noncombatant immunity will vary, "whether consciously or unconsciously, by the claims of necessity." Then *of course* Hiroshima will be regarded as a legitimate military target!

Professor Tucker's comment upon a statement of mine about whether "in the objective order" an immediate effect of action is "incidental" or essential to the action's thrust and intention is: "This is clearly a matter of *quantity* then—of objective consequences" (p. 29; n. 21). Again a palpable error—and moreover one made without first investigating thoroughly the meaning of "incidentality" proposed by the doctrine in question.

There is further confusion for want of doctrinal clarity. "Ordinarily," Tucker begins without noticing that the terms of *bellum justum* are *not* the terms of ordinary language, "we regard a *certain* effect as a means to an end if that end cannot be secured without this effect, if the realization of the one is dependent, and is known to be dependent, upon the occurrence of the other" (p. 30). This statement (which might pass muster if we stress the words *dependent*) is then used to support the conclusion that the death of the innocent "in the course of attacking a military objective is as much a means as is the destruction of the military objective." The latter effect "could not be secured without" destroying a great number of lives; but this fact, if unavoidable, does not make their deaths "as much a means." "Where," writes Tucker, "the one effect, destruction of the military objective, is a means to the end of victory in war, the other effect, the death and injury of noncombatants, is indirectly a means. . . ." The notation upon this sentence should be "So far, so good," provided you know the meaning of "indirectly a means," which is anyway not a good expression for the thought. But then Professor Tucker discloses that he did not know the meaning of "indirectly a means" of victory, by going on to say that the other effect, the death and injury of noncombatants, is "*directly* a means to the end of destroying the military

88

objective." It was not; rather were the civilian deaths incidental, however foreseeable, to the destruction of the military target which was the direct means of victory. Unless, of course, the commander was going about unjustly getting bonus-civil-damage construed as a means of victory. But we could not even know this without knowing the meaning of direct, deliberate attack in distinction from unavoidable, foreseen, collateral damage!

Both effects must be considered as means, we are told. There is in this paragraph, it is true, reference to the notion of "intent" as voiding (Tucker says avoiding) this conclusion. In this reference Professor Tucker shows an awareness that intention is not synonymous with wish or desire in ordinary language or in the terminology of *bellum justum.* "We may not wish or desire something to happen, yet may intend it to happen." The direct killing of combatants may be an example of this. But then Professor Tucker substitutes for the confusion of intent with desire another confusion—of intent with *foreknowledge.* We may not wish a consequence, he writes; but "even so, we intend this consequence if we know that it will result from a certain action and nevertheless take this action." This is simply a grave error in both psychological and moral analysis—and poor reporting of the *bellum justum* doctrine if that is still under scrutiny. "To intend," we are told, "means to have in mind as something to be done or brought about." Something *to be done,* yes. But whether to have in mind something *to be brought about* is synonymous with intending it depends altogether upon how this is envisioned to be brought about. It depends upon knowing the meaning of intentional aims.

The footnote to this paragraph (p. 30; n. 22) contains an acknowledgment that there is a significant distinction to be drawn between "positively intending" the one effect and "indirectly intending" the other effect. This might be enough to permit Tucker his own use of language if he concluded only that *in this sense only* both effects are "intended." Instead he claims too much: "Objectively, we still intend the one effect *just as much* as we intend the other effect" (italics added). Likewise one can almost but not finally permit him his language about "means": "[The indirect means] too is a means, though it is a means that may be distinguished from the means that is directly intended or positively permitted." This statement shows both an understanding of the traditional doctrine and seems to acknowledge the importance of some of its cardinal distinctions in the analysis of just action in war. To press on in the right direction calls for eliminating the use of the expression "indirectly intended" and "indirectly a means." Where Professor Tucker says "indirectly intended," the doctrine under scrutiny says "*un*intended but indirectly *done.*" In any case, with some demurrer over the language used, the paragraph which begins on p. 29 (except for its last sentence) is a correct statement of the doctrine of just conduct. One is bewildered by the degree of Tucker's endorsement of it!

Tucker prosecutes the war against the moralist's verdict that one should never do or intend wrong that good may come into the citadel of attacks *upon combatants*. This must, it seems, not only be done but also judged to be evil, for there to be statecraft. Are we to "positively intend" the death of combatants; is this a "good effect"? The upshot of these questions for Tucker's argument is again to make both of the effects of a military action equally *means* (the one "positively permitted," the other "reluctantly permitted") to the repulsion of injustice which alone can or should be "positively intended" as an ultimate end. This preys off a further confusion between the ultimate or ulterior end or goal and the immediate effects, which alone are in question in the analysis of the nature of present intent and action. Still, Tucker will have to make up his mind whether he means to say that the positive or reluctant permission or intention or doing (whatever the language he finally adopts) of these effects as means is *right* because of the ultimate end, or *wrong* because of the killing and destruction. His view of statecraft would seem to entail the former, but his *bellum contra bellum justum* requires him to say the latter, in order to undercut the ethical verdict that it is never right to do wrong that good may come. In any case, Tucker should know that Christian moralists do not agree with him that only the ulterior effect should be positively intended. Nor do they accept his verdict that to intend and do directly the death of combatants is to do evil that good may come. I myself prefer to say that the intention of combat is the incapacitation of a combatant from doing what he is doing; it is not the killing of a man because he is a man. Others have said instead that the "unjust aggressor" may be killed directly and that to do this is not morally evil. (It undoubtedly is a tragedy and a physical evil; but this is not in question.)

Perhaps it would be helpful to introduce here a few illustrations in which the "scope of the death and injury" remains the same whatever be the intention. From these cases it may be seen that the meaning of the intention can be reasonably and "objectively" discriminated from the "incidentality" of other effects falling unavoidably *within* the scope of the destruction. From them we can also see the *importance* of making this distinction even in cases in which the objective

90

damage remains the same. This will prove that, so far as the theory under discussion is concerned, it is incorrect to define what is intended or what is the means among the manifold effects of action in terms of the objective consequences.

An obstetrician has two women as patients. Both have cancer of the uterus requiring prompt surgical action to remove it. One is pregnant, the other is not.

In both cases it is possible to know the intention of the surgical action. Whether the death of the fetus is directly intended or is beside the intention is clearly *not* determined by the scope of the injury. It is not a matter of quantity. The death of the fetus is *not* a means to saving the mother's life simply because this end cannot be secured without that effect. Nor should it be said that the fetal death is *as much a means* as the destruction of the cancerous uterus, which is the legitimate surgical objective. The doctor does not intend that consequence simply because he knows that it will result from his surgery and nevertheless performs the operation. To have in mind the death of the fetus that will be brought about is *not* his intention. He does *not* intend the one effect as much as he intends the other effect. Unless of course he was going about getting bonus-fetal-damage. We could not determine whether he was or was not meaning to kill the fetus without first knowing the meaning of the direct intention and thrust of proper surgery in this instance. The other case, of the non-pregnant cancerous uterus, shows that this discrimination can be made rationally even in the case of the pregnant woman. In both cases the means of "victory" was the destruction of the diseased uterus, and not also, in the one case, the foreseeable collateral, "incidental" death of the fetus.

The intention of combat and the direct of action is the incapacitation of a combatant, not the killing of a man. *Objection:* He is killed in any case. The "scope" of the injury is the same. The consequence is the same. *Reply:* Yes, but the importance of distinguishing the main thrust of an act of combat from the unavoidable, foreseeable attendant killing of a man even when these produce the same objective event becomes manifestly clear when one asks about the treatment to be justly accorded soldiers who incapacitate themselves as combatants and take themselves out of the war by surrendering. The rule of practice that captured soldiers are not to be killed, and which protects them from gross mistreatment, is a dictate of the justice *inherent* in the conduct of war as a barely human enterprise. This is a regulative principle, a rule of civilized warfare itself. Its bearing upon the conduct of war may not be that captured soldiers ought never to

91

be killed (in fluid, jungle situations in which the "noncombatant" is liable to return quickly to the status of combatant, there being no stockades in which to insure that he will remain a non-warrior.) The bearing of this rule of practice in war may be instead the requirement that every effort be made to implement this limit upon the killing in the entire shape, manner and "institutions" mounted in the conduct of war. This illustration should also serve to indicate something that is too often forgotten when one hears ethicists discussing the moral dimensions of the political use of violence. The upshot is never mainly the definition of culpable individual acts or agents—defining "sin" and making "sinners"—but rather the criticism of institutions and practices. Thus is *bellum justum* a theory of statecraft.

The "incidentality" of killing the man to stopping the combatant is not determined by objective consequences or by the scope of the death. The incapacitation of a combatant is the means, not the other effect without which this cannot be secured. One need *not* intend this other consequence he knows will result beside the intention and beside the prime objective of combat, if, knowing this, he nevertheless engages in combat. The case of the surrendered soldier shows this clearly to be the case, whatever may be the vagaries and furies of men. Justice in the treatment of the man after surrender helps us to see the discrimination to be made in analyzing the difference between "killing in war" and "murder." This shows that the distinction between objectives is *there,* and can be drawn.

During World War II, some of the prominent leaders of world Judaism tried to persuade the Allies to bomb all of Hitler's concentration camps and extermination ovens, even though this would certainly kill all of the inmates at the time of the action. They reasoned that more innocent victims would be saved in the time that would elapse before the camps could be reconstructed and their genocidal work be going again, than lives would be lost "incidental" to destroying the target-camps and personnel that should justly have been repressed. Would this have been to do evil that good may come? Prescinding from whether the proposed action would, or would likely enough, have achieved the proportion of effectiveness and value expected (that would be one of the reasons for declaring that this should not be done), would such strikes against the concentration camps have been deliberate, direct attacks upon the innocent no less than upon the furnaces?

The answer to this is clearly, No. This shows that one does not deduce intention from the consequences. In this case, also, whether the deaths are directly intended or beside the intention cannot be determined by the scope of the death and destruction. Incidentality is not a matter of quantity, even where the quantity remains the same and cannot be altered by any difference in the intention. The death of the inmates was not a part of the means to the end in view simply because that end could not be secured without this effect. Their deaths were clearly *not* as much a means as the destruction of the target-furnaces. An immediate consequence known to result would not have been the intention of this action. To have in mind something that will unavoidably be brought about is not the same as aiming at it. No one would actually intend the secondary effect just as much as he intends and directs the other effect upon its target by the action in question. Unless of course there were latent anti-Semites in the Allied high command who might have intended to get bonus-inmate-damage. But (apart from character-analysis) we could not reasonably and objectively tell whether this was so or not unless it is possible to know first the meaning of deliberate, direct attack upon legitimate military targets. The fact that the action would have been carried out exactly as proposed had there been intelligence of a certain lucky day on which the camps would be empty of inmates provides in this instance a clarifying test-case like the woman who was not pregnant and the combatant who has surrendered in the foregoing illustrations.

These are hard cases, deliberately chosen because they are hard cases, or rather because they demonstrate the determinate meaning of the intention of an action without varying the scope of the destruction.

The importance of this analysis in the theory of *bellum justum* is, of course, that without the principle of discrimination in one's doctrine of statecraft and in the conduct of war there is no reason to limit the scope of the destruction and increments in the use of violence by any reference to whether the "targets" are populations or not. It would be a proportion of effectiveness alone that gave preference to the one or the other. This world already knows what that means, even if there seems to be some considerable difficulty in coming to know the meaning of "aiming discriminately" among the laws of war.

No less a realist than Herman Kahn can tell the difference, without preferring one to the other, between war-plans and military strikes that aim to get bonus-civil-damage as part of the means of victory and one that aims at counter-force-plus-avoidance of as much civil damage as possible. This does not seem to be a distinction that can even be made in the minds of men if Professor Tucker's replacing definition of intention is correct. It should in any case be clear who has emasculated the doctrine of *bellum justum* in the course of interpreting it.

V

There remains the question whether *bellum justum*, correctly understood, provides a *viable* theory of statecraft at the point of the state's use of violence in modern war.

Tucker makes an initially profoundly true contention that no matter what the higher values the state serves, and despite the hierarchy of values in human political communities, a "realistic" statecraft nevertheless holds true if only the state is a *necessary* condition to these higher human goods. The state's "self," territorial integrity and independence may not be the supreme good. The state may be only a *conditional* instrumental value, inferior to all the rest. However, the state is a *necessary* condition to the higher values it serves. Therefore, when the chips are down, it is *as if* the state were the supreme value. Provided the state is a necessary condition, the state is *functionally* the supreme value. A *necessary* condition of all the other political goods must be protected at all costs. This the state will do, and should do for the sake of those superior, unconditional values to which it is a necessary condition. The fact that in politics there are values superior to the safety of the state does not, therefore, open the way to any moral limitation upon the practice of statecraft. Precisely for the sake of those other values which the state serves and to which it is an indispensable condition, the safety of the state must be insured. Thus, the basic value is more important than all the rest, precisely because it is a necessary condition to all the rest. As an argument, this seems a clincher!

However, the requirement that statecraft insure the safety of the state needs to be correctly understood even at this initial and most fundamental level. Tucker seems to believe that what seems true when the chips are down proves that the practice of statecraft is a closed circle. He seems to believe that acceptance of the principle that each individual should be considered a moral finality in himself would not require a modification but *the end* of statecraft. Instead, the premise that when the chips are down there are no "wandering nations" stems precisely from the fact that only man has a moral finality in himself, and the state does not. Since the state is *only* a conditional value having no moral finality in itself, the safety of the state should be insured precisely for the sake of generations of men who do have moral finality and for the sake of the unconditional ends constituent of the common good.

94

Professor Tucker judges that a realistic statecraft requires that the moral finality resident in individual men be dismissed from politics. He should have concluded instead that the first requirement which this principle itself places upon the conduct of statecraft is that a nation's "self" be defended for the sake of finalities it has not.

This is enough to open the question whether acceptance of the principle that each individual has moral finality in himself would in other respects put an end to statecraft. Perhaps Tucker has simply misstated what is entailed by the moral finality resident in men, and found *this* to be incompatible with statecraft.

The next step is to bring into attention those many situations in which the state is a *condition*, even a *necessary* condition, to the attainment of higher political goals, but is not a *sufficient* condition to their attainment. From this the correct inference is that the state must do *more* than preserve its own safety, or that more must be done in the political community if there is to be sufficient condition for the unconditional ends to be realized in the common life. There may even be other *necessary* conditions besides the safety and independence of the state. The proper conduct of statecraft, then, will require the provision of not only all the necessary conditions but also the sufficient conditions, and all the *necessary and sufficient* conditions in directing the community to the common good.

I presume that Tucker would not disagree with this, provided only that the safety of the state is not removed from among the necessary conditions. He need not even disagree that, in view of the requirement that the conditions be sufficient, nation-state statecraft entails abundant and urgent concern for the health of the international system and the common good of mankind.

The final step, however, brings us to the crux of the matter. The fact is that not only is the state an insufficient condition in the privative sense, requiring that far *more* be done to make the conditions sufficient than preserving the state's "self" and independence by wielding quantitative increments of force. The fact is that the modern state is positively insufficient, not merely negatively so. Something *other* may need to be done. Because of the nature of the weapons into the use of which the politics of the nation-state may extend, "necessities of state" may quite readily contradict, frustrate and destroy those very values which the state exists to serve. The state as necessary condition may become destructive of the goals to which it is ordinarily a condition.

"Reasons of state" are valid only so long as the state itself has reason. Not that the nation-state has automatically ceased to be necessary. The dilemma is rather that the state while continuing to be in some sense still necessary may in the pursuit of its own safety today readily contradict those very goals for which it is necessary and which alone justify its "reasons of state." We must now say that the state's *raison d'état* depend for justification upon the state's *raison d'être*, which brings us again to the goods the state is supposed to serve. Rather, this was always the truth of the matter; today it is only evident beyond question. The argument that, since the state is a necessary condition, the safety of the state *functions* as the supreme value even if it is not, can no longer serve when that will likely *contradict* all the values it conditions. Only inflexible political reasoning can today continue along this course.

We must say not only that *more* needs to be done for there to be sufficient conditions for the attainment of the goals of politics. That should have been said all along. Instead we evidently must now say that *something other* must be done than simply to preserve the safety of the state when to do so precisely de-conditions, contradicts and would destroy the values and finalities which alone give warrant to the state's conditional value. It can no longer be argued that because the state is a necessary condition its safety *functions* as the supreme value. In an age when the state in seeking its safety can prove positively *dis*functional as a condition (and not only insufficient), resort must be made again directly to those unconditional values and finalities which before or ordinarily warrant the exercise of statecraft *as if* the state were the supreme value. We must proceed again to adduce from these higher values and finalities better insight into the proper conduct of statecraft, along the same route by which we initially derived the basic moral reason for the state's "reasons of state," the functionally supreme necessity of its necessities, the choiceworthiness of choosing its safety before all else. The supreme ends of political community have actually become conditional, and necessarily so, and conditional to the safety of the state, in an age when the routine pursuit of these goals through the safety of the state may destroy both these values themselves and every condition for the successful pursuit of them. This is the *bouleversement* the nuclear age has accomplished!

There are two ways to make renewed appeal to the goals of political community and to the finalities resident in men in reconstructing the politics of the nuclear age and our understanding of statecraft.

One way is to appeal to the goals or ends or values served by statecraft and ask again what this requires in and of the conditions. This will mean severely but prudently limiting the means it would ever be just to employ to save the state, in accordance with the principle of proportion, a proportion of effectiveness and of value. This has been the pressure to perfect institutions of an international order, correcting the structural defects of the nation-state system. This is the impulse behind endeavors to proscribe in customary international law, or by agreement, all but defensive wars, first use of nuclears, etc. This was the main emphasis of modern Roman Catholic (Papal) teachings until the Vatican Council added to these limitations of prudence and proportion upon the exercise of statecraft its own additional and most solemn condemnation of aiming indiscriminately at the destruction of entire cities with their populations. (The latter is a definition of right conduct in war that follows from renewed appeal to the finalities resident in man himself.)

This is also the argument of many political scientists, notably Hans Morgenthau; and, resting as this does on a principle plainly inherent in the exercise of statecraft, I do not suppose Tucker would at all disagree. (In fact one of his charges against proponents of *bellum justum* is that they seem to him to be morally insensitive by justifying more destructiveness under the principle of discrimination than prudence or proportion would allow.) "I would say without qualification," writes Morgenthau, "that a thermonuclear war, however begun, cannot be justified on moral grounds." The reason he gives for this verdict is as follows: "The moral evil inherent in any act of violence is mitigated by the end the act serves. . . . Nuclear war destroys the saving impact that good ends exert upon evil means. For nuclear war is not only irrational, in that it destroys the very end for which it is waged, but, by dint of that irrationality, it is also immoral in that the destruction of the end for which it is waged renders its moral justification impossible."[5] In short, thermonuclear war removes the reason from reasons of state, and destroys everything that ever gave warrant to necessities of state.

The other way—an additional, not an alternative way—to renew appeal to qualities of political justice that today have become functionally fundamental to the proper exercise of statecraft is to attend to the finality in man himself which politics should serve and not contradict even in acts of war. This is the principle of discrimination forbidding acts of war aimed indiscriminately at populations as a means of "victory" or to save the state. The question is: does this afford needed insight into the meaning of statecraft that is both

---

[5] *Christianity and Crisis*, Dec. 11, 1961, p. 223.

97

proper and relevant in the world of today, or would it require, as Tucker believes, the abandonment of statecraft?

The prohibition of organized direct attack upon populations has become an evident, constituent element of statecraft today. This has become evident in the concept of "central" war for which the nuclear nations are organized. All along, direct killing of innocent non-combatants was wrong. Moreover, while wrong it was always *beside* the main thrust or plan of war, since (however much injustice was done in war's conduct in the past) this was peripheral and it required too much muscle to fight wars most or all of the time by civilian genocidal acts. Today such acts have become easily within reach of modern military technology (nuclear and non-nuclear). Therefore, another principle besides proportion has been laid bare in the anatomy of statecraft and in the use of force as an instrument of policy. This must be both discriminate and proportionate. Today the validity of *bellum justum* as a theory of statecraft has been thrust upon us. This is ever more evident to everyone except the defenders of old-line reasons of state and the pragmatic policy-makers and crisis-manipulators.

The small but important virtue of the limitation which the principle of discrimination imposes upon statecraft, or rather reveals to be in the nature of a proper statecraft, is the absolute prohibition of total war in all its forms. This can never be an apt exercise of state-craft. The principle of discrimination discloses the final irrationality and immorality of pure "rationality of irrationality" policies, tit-for-tat city-exchanges played out to discover who is more resolutely determined to do any and everything for the safety of the state.

Tucker invokes political prudence which begins to operate much lower in the scale of violence to place limits upon the use of force. He then benefits by bringing this against proponents of *bellum justum* who have sought to show how the prohibition of deliberate, direct attacks upon civil life, taken alone, would work out in practice in the direction of political life in the nuclear age (and in this age of subversive warfare—which is total war at the subconventional level). He forgets that *bellum justum* includes also the requirement of political prudence or the proportionate use of force no less than does his own theory of statecraft, and that discrimination is never to be taken alone.

As a consequence his readers are apt to forget that, when taken alone, prudence and proportion, which begin to impose earlier limits, have in the spectrum of violence thereafter nowhere to stop, or no reason for stopping anywhere. They are apt to forget that Tucker's theory of statecraft would not rule out the possibility of going to city-exchanges for reasons of state, to preserve the state's "self," integrity and independence in however self-contradictory a fashion.

This may only be to say that central violations of the principle of discrimination have been proved in the nature of modern warfare to be the highest form of imprudence and a political use of violence that cannot be proportionate to any good to come of it. To say this is not to say that war aimed indiscriminately upon populations is wrong only *because* disproportionate in means to ends. It is to say rather that this would be wrong for *both* reasons. It is to say that this would be wrong because it is a direct violation of the finality resident in men *and* that no good but only extensive political evil can ever come of it.

It is difficult to understand why Tucker is such a purist in moral reasoning (and therefore a purist in his theory of statecraft) that he demands to be shown that one should never wage war indiscriminately even though a very great deal of good will come from such a strategy. This is simply not the way the nations are presently organized for war. The fact is that they are organized for war in ways that cannot fail to destroy both the state's conditional value and all other conditional and unconditioned values in the political life of mankind. There has taken place a *convergence* of the two principles in placing limits upon meaningful statecraft. This is altogether different from saying that acts of war aimed indiscriminately are wrong *because* only the mutual destruction of states can come from it and not their safety. Because of this fact, no doubt, practical men are being driven to the roots again, to renew direct appeals to fundamental norms governing the use of force, in order to discern in the distinction between legitimate and illegitimate military targets the meaning of legitimate statecraft today. Mankind's slow and tortuous discovery of any political values or the achievement of insight into how to act rightly in our historical existence has always been by discovering these things to be *incarnate*.

We are not apt without such appeals to the ultimate finalities to begin to put nuclear weapons in a class by themselves as weapons intended to be not used, or not used over primarily population objectives, or to put them in a class by themselves as weapons intended to be used only in intentional non-use for deterrence's sake. Below this in the theory of *bellum justum* are all the limits of disproportion on which alone Tucker and Morganthau seem to want to rely, as in the main did Papal teachings before the Vatican Council. The peoples and nations in the modern world, however, are not apt to proceed further in transforming *jus ad bellum* into *jus contra bellum* without more than this, without also the force of *jus in bello* (noncombatant immunity) upon political consciences.

There is a final point that is so obvious that it should not be necessary to call attention to it. Of course more is needed than aptitude in perceiving the "natural justice" which governs the political use of violence. More is needed than political prudence determining *jus ad bellum* or *jus contra bellum* and determining, in the last resort, *jus in bello* in so far as this means economy in the use of force or threats. More also is needed than *jus in bello* forbidding the fighting of the central indiscriminate war that is possible today. More is needed than *jus in bello* requiring instead that such use of these weapons be intended never to be done; and that their deterrent use be subdued until either this intended use is taken out of national deterrent-systems or, if that is not possible, a radical political reconstruction of the present international system is accomplished that can exercise statecraft in a new way stripped of the necessity of ever intending to use violence massively against populations.

In addition to the tests and impulses to justice that are inherent to the nature and meaning of a proper statecraft, there is also need for all sorts of "positive laws" and agreements and institutions among men and nations that go beyond all this in specificity, and place further limits upon the exercise of statecraft in this age of violence. There is really no reason to be found in the justice of war itself for forbidding aggressive war and allowing only the right of self-defense, or for forbidding the use of a certain weapons system as such. Still there may be needed additional rules of practice in the building of a more orderly international system, and some of these rules of practice may be additional specifications of the requirement of prudence. Today there may be growing consensus or a "customary international law" forbidding *first* use of nuclear weapons, or any use of any nuclears. Perhaps explicit international agreements should be made formalizing such customary international law on these and many other matters.

It has always been an assumption of political theory in the Western world that, while there are moral principles in the "state of nature" among the nations that are regulative of resort to war, men can nevertheless improve on the state of nature. Theirs is a task of law-*making* and institution-building. We are not apt to do this, I would argue, if we are persuaded that there is no law to be *found* in the state of nature, in the nature and meaning of statecraft and regulative of its proper exercise. But the final point to be made is the need, even so, for the further specification of law and institutions in the international order.

It is odd that anyone should suppose that a proponent of *bellum justum* in attempting to revive some memory of the minimal requirements upon the conduct of politics even in a state of nature among the nations should, because of the justifications and limitations he *finds* among the laws of war, be supposed to be lacking in cognizance of the need for further specifications of *jus ad* (*contra*) *bellum* and *jus in bello*, or that he should be accused of denying the need for a manifold work of political reason and action in the making of law and in constructing new formations of the political life of mankind that will help to moderate and proportion political means more rationally to political ends. It is not *bellum justum* that has no room for positivism in statecraft. It is rather an entirely positivistic viewpoint has no room for justice among the constituent elements of statecraft.

HIEBERT LIBRARY

3 6877 00204 7107

U
21.2
.T8